T0345207

SECURE, RESILIENT, AND AGILE SOFTWARE DEVELOPMENT

SECURE, RESILIENT, AND AGILE SOFTWARE DEVELOPMENT

Mark S. Merkow, CISSP, CISM, CSSLP

CRC Press
Taylor & Francis Group
Boca Raton London New York

CRC Press is an imprint of the
Taylor & Francis Group, an **informa** business
AN AUERBACH BOOK

CRC Press
Taylor & Francis Group
6000 Broken Sound Parkway NW, Suite 300
Boca Raton, FL 33487-2742

© 2020 by Taylor & Francis Group
CRC Press is an imprint of Taylor & Francis Group, an Informa business

No claim to original U.S. Government works

Printed on acid-free paper

International Standard Book Number-13: 978-0-367-33259-4 (Hardback)

**Visit the Taylor & Francis Web site at
http://www.taylorandfrancis.com**

**and the CRC Press Web site at
http://www.crcpress.com**

Trademarks Used in This Publication

Adobe® is a registered trademark of Adobe, Inc., in San Jose, CA.

Alert Logic® is a registered trademark of Alert Logic Inc., in Houston, TX

Amazon Web Services® is a registered trademark of Amazon Technologies, Inc., in Seattle, WA.

AppScan® and IBM® are registered trademarks of International Business Machines Corporation, in Armonk, NY.

Atlassian® and Jira® are registered trademarks of Atlassian Pty Ltd., Sydney, Australia.

Azure® is a registered trademark of Microsoft Corporation, in Redmond, WA (on hold pending further action as of 2019/09).

Barracuda® is a registered trademark of Barracuda Networks Inc., in Campbell, CA.

Cigital® is a registered trademark of Synopsys, Inc., in Mountain View, CA.

Citrix® is a registered trademark of Citrix Systems, Inc.

Contrast Security® is a registered trademark of Contrast Security, Inc., in Los Altos, CA.

CSSLP® and (ISC)²® are registered trademarks of International Information Systems Security Certification Consortium, Inc., in Clearwater, FL.

CVE® is a registered trademark and CWE™ is a trademark of MITRE Corporation, in McLean, VA.

Dell® and Dell® EMC® are registered trademarks of Dell Inc. or its subsidiaries.

Ethereum® is a registered trademark of Stiftung Ethereum (Foundation Ethereum).

F5 Silverline® is a registered trademark of F5 Networks Inc., in Seattle, WA.

Fortify® is a registered trademark of EntIT Software LLC, in Sunnyvale, CA.

GCP® is a registered trademark and Google™ is a trademark of Google, Inc., in Mountain View, CA.

ImmuniWeb® is a globally registered trademark owned by High Tech Bridge SA, in Geneva, Switzerland.

Imperva® is a registered trademark of Imperva Inc. in Redwood City, CA.

ISACA® is a registered trademark of Information Systems Audit and Control Association, Inc., in Schaumburg, IL.

IriusRisk® is a registered trademark of Continuum Security, SL, in Spain.

Jama Connect™ is a trademark of Jama Software, in Portland, OR.

Kubernetes® is a registered trademark of The Linux Foundation, in San Francisco, CA.

LinkedIn® is a registered trademark of LinkedIn Corporation, in Sunnyvale, CA.

Microsoft® is a registered trademark of Microsoft Corporation, in Redmond, WA.

NICERC™ is a trademark of National Integrated Cyber Education Research Center, in Bossier City, LA.

Offensive Security® is a registered trademark of Offensive Security Limited, in George Town, Grand Cayman.

OWASP is designated as non-final office action issued (clarification needed as of 2019/09).

Qualys® is a registered trademark of Qualys Inc., in Foster City, CA.

Radware® is a registered trademark of Radware, in Mahwah, NJ.

ScienceSoft® is a registered trademark of ScienceSoft USA Corporation, in McKinney, TX.

SonarQube™ is a trademark of SonarSource SA, in Switzerland.

Sonatype® is a trademark of Sonatype Inc., in Fulton, MD.

Synopsys® and Synopsys Coverity® are registered trademarks of Synopsys, Inc., in the U.S. and/or other countries.

ThreatModeler® is a registered trademark of ThreatModeler Software, Inc., in Jersey City, NJ.

Wallarm® is a registered trademark of Wallarm Inc., in San Francisco, CA.

Dedication

This book is dedicated to the next generation of application security
professionals to help alleviate the struggle to reverse the curses
of defective software, no matter where it shows up.

Contents

Preface

This book was written from the perspective of someone who began his software security career in 2005, long before we knew much about it. Making all the rookie mistakes one tends to make without any useful guidance quickly turns what's supposed to be a helpful process into one that creates endless chaos and lots of angry people. After a few rounds of these rookie mistakes, it finally dawned on me that we're going about it all wrong. Software security is actually a human factor issue, not a technical or process issue alone. Throwing technology into an environment that expects people to deal with it but failing to prepare them technically and psychologically with the knowledge and skills needed is a certain recipe for bad results.

Think of this book as a collection of best practices and effective implementation recommendations that are proven to work. I've taken the boring details of software security theory out of the discussion as much as possible to concentrate on practical applied software security for practical people.

This is as much a book for your personal benefit as it is for your organization's benefit. Professionals who are skilled in secure and resilient software development and related tasks are in tremendous and growing demand, and the market will remain that way for the foreseeable future. As you integrate these ideas into your daily duties, your value increases to your company, your management, your community, and your industry.

Secure, Resilient, and Agile Software Development was written with the following people in mind:

- AppSec architects and program managers in information security organizations
- Enterprise architecture teams with application development focus
- Scrum teams
  - Scrum masters
  - Engineers/developers

- ○ Analysts
- ○ Architects
- ○ Testers
- DevOps teams
- Product owners and their management
- Project managers
- Application security auditors
- Agile coaches and trainers
- Instructors and trainers in academia and private organizations

How This Book Is Organized

- Chapter 1 brings the state of software development up to date after the tsunami of changes that have flipped software development and application security practices on their head since 2010, when I co-authored *Secure and Resilient Software: Requirements, Test Cases, and Testing Methods.*
- Chapter 2 takes a detailed look at the Agile and Scrum software development methodology to explore how security controls need to change in light of an entirely new paradigm on how software is developed and how software is used.
- Chapter 3 focuses on ways to educate everyone who has a hand in any software development project with appropriate and practical skills to Build Security In. We look at ways of influencing development teams to espouse software security in their day-to-day activities, establishing a role-based curriculum for everyone, suggestions on how to roll out training, and ways to "keep the drumbeat alive" all year long through outreach and events.
- Chapters 4 looks at the specification steps of new or altered software with ways to incorporate security controls and other nonfunctional requirements (NRFs) into user stories that bring to life the concepts of "shift left" and Building Security In. This chapter examines 15 families of nonfunctional requirements and 11 families of application security controls.
- Chapter 5 moves into foundational and fundamental principles for secure application design. It covers important concepts, techniques, and design goals to meet well-understood acceptance criteria on features an application must implement.
- Chapter 6 examines how the design sprint is adapted for proper consideration of security and other NFRs and ways to conduct threat modeling, application risk analysis, and practical remediation while the design is still malleable.
- Chapter 7 on defensive programming includes information on the Common Weaknesses Enumeration (CWE™), the OWASP Top 10 (2017), and some ways to address the *fundamental scourge* of application security vulnerabilities—failure to sanitize inputs.
- Chapter 8 is focused on white box application analysis with sprint-based activities to improve security and quality of an application under development. Static code analysis is covered in depth for context on what these tools do and the assumptions they use for operating.

- Chapter 9 looks at black box or grey box analysis techniques and tools for testing a running version of an application for software or quality shortcomings.
- Chapter 10 is focused on techniques and activities to help transform the DevOps process into a DevSecOps process with appropriate controls, metrics, and monitoring processes.
- Chapter 11 looks at two popular software maturity and metrics models for helping you determine the effectiveness and maturity of your secure development program.
- Chapter 12 takes a survey of the frontier in which software use is expanding. It covers topics including the Internet of Things (IoT), AI, machine learning, blockchains, microservices, APIs, containers, and more.
- Chapter 13 closes the book with a call to action to help you gain access to education, certification programs, and industry initiatives to which you can contribute.

Each chapter logically builds on prior chapters to help you paint a complete picture of what's required for secure, resilient, and Agile application software as you learn how to implement environment-specific, effective controls and management processes that will make you the envy of your peers!

About the Author

Mark S. Merkow, CISSP, CISM, CSSLP, works at WageWorks in Tempe, Arizona, leading application security architecture and engineering efforts in the office of the CISO. Mark has over 40 years of experience in IT in a variety of roles, including application development, systems analysis and design, security engineering, and security management. Mark holds a Master of Science in Decision and Information Systems from Arizona State University (ASU), a Master of Education in Distance Education from ASU, and a Bachelor of Science in Computer Information Systems from ASU. In addition to his day job, Mark engages in a number of extracurricular activities, including consulting, course development, online course instruction, and book writing.

Mark has authored or co-authored 17 books on IT and has been a contributing editor to four others. Mark remains very active in the information security community, working in a variety of volunteer roles for the Phoenix Chapter of (ISC)²®, ISACA®, and OWASP. You can find Mark's LinkedIn® profile at: linkedin.com/in/markmerkow

Chapter 1

Today's Software Development Practices Shatter Old Security Practices

In the decade since *Secure and Resilient Software: Requirements, Test Cases, and Testing Methods*[1] was published, the world of software development has flipped on its head, shed practices from the past, brought about countless changes, and revolutionized how software is designed, developed, maintained, operated, and managed.

These changes crept in slowly at first, then gained momentum and have since overtaken most of what we "know" about software development and the security tried-and-true methods that we've relied on and implemented over the years. Involvement from application security (appsec) professionals—if they happened at all—happened WAY too late, before executive decisions were already made to supplant old practices and the ink was already dried on contracts with companies hired to make the change.

This late (or nonexistent) involvement in planning how to address security hobbles appsec practitioners who are forced to bargain, barter, or somehow convince development teams that they simply cannot ignore security. Compound this problem with the nonstop pace of change, and appsec professionals must abandon old "ways" and try to adapt controls to a moving target. Furthermore, the risks with all-new attack surfaces (such as autonomous vehicles), reliance on the Internet of Things (IoT), and software that comes to life with kinetic activity can place actual human lives in real danger of injury or death.

Although we may have less work on our hands to convince people that insecure software is a clear and present danger, appsec professionals have to work **much** harder to get everyone on board to apply best practices that we are confident will work.

A decade ago, we were striving to help appsec professionals to convince development organizations to—minimally—address software security in every phase of development, and for the most part over the decade, we saw that far more attention is being paid to appsec within the software development lifecycle (SDLC), but now we're forced to adapt how we do things to new processes that may be resistant to any changes that slow things down, while the risks and impacts of defective software increase exponentially.

Here's the definition of software resilience that we'll use throughout the book. This definition is an adaptation of the National Infrastructure Advisory Council (NIAC) definition of infrastructure resilience:

> *Software resilience is the ability to reduce the magnitude and/or duration of disruptive events. The effectiveness of a resilient application or infrastructure software depends upon its ability to anticipate, absorb, adapt to, and/or rapidly recover from a potentially disruptive event.*[2]

In this chapter, we're going to survey this new landscape for these changes to update our own models on how to adapt to the Brave New World and maintain software security, resilience, and agility.

1.1 Over the Waterfall

New paradigms have rapidly replaced the Waterfall model of software development that we've used since the beginning of the software age. Agile and Scrum SDLCs have all but displaced the rigorous (and sometime onerous) activities, and most certainly displaced the notion of "phase containment," which appsec professionals have counted on as a reliable means to prevent defects from creeping into subsequent phases.

This new landscape includes Agile/Scrum, DevOps, continuous integration/deployment (CI/CD), and the newest revolution working its way in, site reliability engineering (SRE). To adapt to these changes, we need to understand how the rigor we've put into Waterfall-based projects and processes has been swept away by the tsunami of change that demands more software, faster and cheaper.

Changes in the software *development* paradigm forces change in the software *security* paradigm, which MUST work hand-in-hand with what development teams are expected to do. While we typically had a shot at inspecting software for security issues at the end of the development cycle (because of phase containment), this control point no longer exists. The new paradigm we had to adopt is called *"shift left,"* preserving the notion that there are still phases in the SDLC, while recognizing the fact that there aren't.

1.2 What Is Agile?

In essence, Agile and Scrum are based on the philosophy that software takes on a life of its own, constantly being improved, extended, and enhanced, and these changes can be delivered in hours, rather than weeks, months, or years.

Let's take a look at the overall scope of the Agile/Scrum process, as shown in Figure 1.1. This diagram encapsulates all the processes described by Scrum and some suggested time frames showing how it compresses time into digestible bites that continue to produce software. Some new roles are also indicated (e.g., product owner and Scrum master), and teams are composed of ALL the roles you formerly find on separate teams using Waterfall methods. This means that one team is composed of the roles responsible for analysis, design, coding, testing, coordination, and ongoing delivery as new features are added, changes are made, or defects removed. It also means that work is not tossed over the wall to the next person in line to do "something." The team is responsible for all the effort and results.

A minimally viable product (MVP) is the first release of a new software application that's considered "bare bones" but has sufficient functionality for release to the market before the competition releases their own version. While the actions are not shown in each sprint, they typically follow the same activities you'd find in the Waterfall model, but with more iterations and fewer phase gates that control when software is tested and released. Software is then changed regularly and is never really considered "complete." This creates severe challenges for appsec.

We'll examine the Agile/Scrum process in depth in Chapter 2 and look inside each sprint to see where security controls can work.

1.3 Shift Left!

Shifting left requires that development teams address software security from the very inception of a project (Build Security In) and in every step along the way

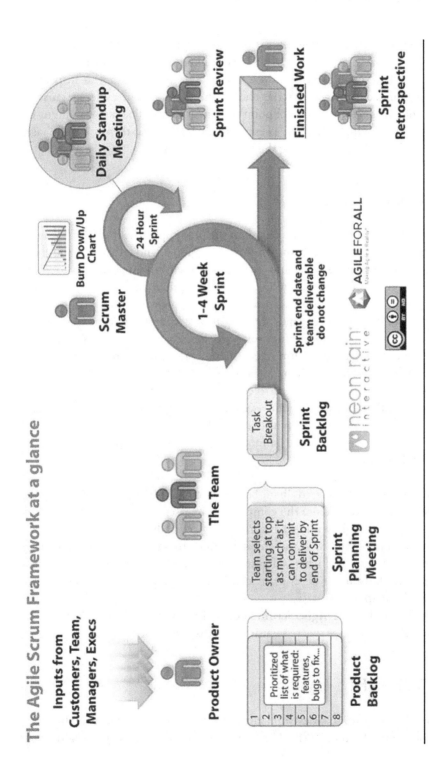

Figure 1.1 Agile/Scrum Framework (*Source*: Neon Rain Interactive, licensed under CC BY-ND 3.0 NZ)

to its manifestation. This means that everyone who has a hand in the specification and development of this new software "product" clearly understands their security obligations and is prepared and able to meet those obligations. Security teams can no longer "do" security for development teams—the teams must be responsible and able to prove they're living up to those expectations. We'll talk about how to make this happen with development team awareness, training, and education in Chapter 3.

Shifting left also requires new ways in how designers create solutions based on the requirements and how they vet those solutions for potential security problems, since they clearly understand that changes in design once an application is developed will cost potentially hundreds of times more than if the defects were caught while architecture and engineering is underway.

Developers are affected because they're not given the luxury of time for extensive testing, as they often had with former practices. Now, developers may release new code all day and see it deployed within minutes, so it's vital that these developers "own" the responsibility for securing it, which means developing it using a defensive programming state of mind. Shifting left in the development activity involves active use—and appropriate response—with security checks built directly into their integrated development environment (IDE)—for example, Visual Studio or Eclipse. Although these checks are on incomplete segments of an overall application, coding provides the first opportunity for security inspection and is needed to continue the cycle of appsec.

Testing presents a major challenge to appsec, because tolerance for long-running tests has all but disappeared. Although it's true that a comprehensive (finished this time) application is needed for comprehensive testing, product managers won't wait anymore while security tests are run, and vulnerable applications may be deployed (ship it now—fix it later). Shifting left in this environment forces security testing to happen incrementally, in what we used to call integration testing—the point in development at which all the elements come together to build as a new version of the software. If the implementation of security testing is done correctly and responsively to the needs of the product managers, it can serve as a control to actually "break" a build and force remediation of defects. We'll discuss this at length in Chapters 10 and 11 on testing.

Taken together, shifting left in the appsec space makes it possible to gain the assurance we need that our applications are *appropriately* secure, but it changes the role of appsec professionals from "doing" appsec to needing to empower everyone who touches software in the SDLC with practical and appropriate knowledge, skills, and abilities.

Although the names and accelerated pace has significantly changed how we deal with appsec, the activities of software development, as we understood them in Waterfall methodologies, are still present. Requirements are still being gathered, designs are still being built, coders are still coding, testers are still testing, and operators are still deploying and managing applications in production. We can apply what we know works to help secure applications in development, but we have to step back and let those who are intimate with the application do the heavy lifting and prove to us that they've done what they needed to do!

At the end of the day, software security is a human factors issue—not a technical issue—and for appsec professionals to succeed in implementing application controls, it's vital to treat the human factor in ways we know work, rather than throwing more tools at the problem.

1.4 Principles First!

Before we dig into the details on how to create and maintain excellence in application security programs, let's cover some enduring principles that we need to live by in everything we do to secure application software and the processes used to create it:

- Secure application development is a PEOPLE issue, not a technical one.
- Every intervention into the SDLC affects people.
- Shift Left within the SDLC as much of the appsec work as you can—the more security work that's performed closest to the point at which defects are introduced is the surest way of eliminating them and preventing "defect creep" from one phase or activity to the next.
- AppSec tools are great but of are questionable use if the people using them don't understand:
  ○ What the tool is telling them
  ○ Why their code is vulnerable
  ○ How their code is vulnerable
  ○ What do to about the vulnerability
- People can only deal with so much change at one time—too many changes all at once to their processes leads to chaos and ultimately rebellion.
- Automate everything that you can (scanning, remediation planning, retesting, etc.).
- There are only so many of us in the information security departments, but thousands of development team staff who need accountability; don't treat security as a punishment or barrier—convince development team members that it empowers them, makes them more valuable as employees and members of the development community, and they'll quickly learn that it does all these things!

1.5 Summary

In Chapter 1, we surveyed the modern-day landscape on how software is developed, operated, and managed to understand the impacts these changes have forced on how we design, develop, and implement control mechansims to assure software security and resilience. We'll begin to explore how appsec professionals can *use* Agile practices to *improve* Agile practices with security controls and how baking in security from the very start is the surest way to gain assurance that your applications can stand up and recover from chronic attacks.

References

1. Merkow, M. and Ragahvan, L. (2011). *Secure and Resilient Software: Requirements, Test Cases, and Testing Methods.* 1st Ed. Auerbach Publications.
2. Critical Infrastructure Resilience Final Report and Recommendations, National Infrastructure Advisory Council. Retrieved June 11, 2019, from http://www.dhs.gov/xlibrary/assets/niac/niac_critical_infrastructure_resilience.pdf

Chapter 2

Deconstructing Agile and Scrum

For purposes of context setting and terminology, we're going to deconstruct the Agile/Scrum development methodology to discover areas in which appsec controls help in securing software in development and also help to control the development methodology itself. We'll look at ways to use Agile to secure Agile.

Let's revisit the overall scope of the Agile/Scrum process, shown in Figure 2.1 (originally Figure 1.1).

There's Agile/Scrum as a formal, strict, tightly controlled process, then there's Agile/Scrum as it's implemented in the real world. Implementation of Agile will vary from the fundamentalist and purist views to various elements that appear as Agile-like processes, and everything in between. It's less important HOW it's implemented in your environment than it is to understand what your specific implementation means to your appsec efforts.

2.1 The Goals of Agile and Scrum

Agile software development refers to software development lifecycle (SDLC) methodologies based on the idea of iterative development, in which requirements and solutions evolve through collaboration between self-organizing, cross-functional teams. Agile development is designed to enable teams to deliver value faster, with greater quality and predictability and greater abilities to respond to change.[1]

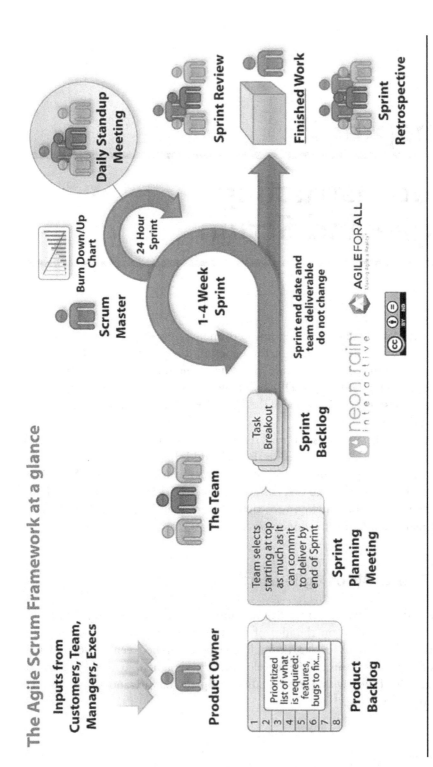

Figure 2.1 Agile/Scrum Framework (*Source:* Neon Rain Interactive, licensed under CC BY-ND 3.0 NZ)

Scrum and Kanban are the dominant implementations of Agile, and Scrum is the one most often found in software development organizations.

2.2 Agile/Scrum Terminology

Here are some common terms and roles found within Agile SDLCs:

Product—the application under development, enhancement, or replacement.

Product Backlog—the list of features or requirements that the product must include. These features are prioritized by the product owner for submission to sprints.

Product Owner—typically from a business unit or business area who becomes responsible for the creation of new products through the specifications (user stories) they create and add to the product backlog. Think of the product owner as the sponsor of the work the team performs overall. Often, the Scrum team and the product owner work in entirely different organizations (a business unit outside of the technology division of the firm).

User Stories—User stories help to shift the focus from *writing* about requirements to *talking* about them.[2] Stories use non-technical language to provide context for the development team and their efforts. After reading a user story, the team knows why they are building what they're building and what value it creates.[3] User stories are added to sprints and "burned down" over the duration of the sprint.

Figure 2.2 depicts an example of a typical user story[4]:

Sprint—a fixed, time-boxed period of time (typically from 2–4 weeks), during which specific prioritized requirements (user stories) are fed in from the product backlog for design or development.

Definition of Done (DoD)—Each Scrum team has its own DoD or consistent acceptance criteria across all user stories. A DoD drives the quality of work and is used to assess when a user story has been completed.

2.3 Agile/Scrum Roles

Scrum role team titles are only relevant in establishing each person's specific expertise, but they don't lock those who are in that role into only performing that activity. Teams are self-organizing, so expertise is shared across the team as

As...	Conditional	I want...	So that...
As an HR Rep	who is authorized to initiate reviews for new employees	I want to be notified when new hires have reached their 90 day mark	so that I can initiate a 90-day review.
As an HR Rep	who has initiated a 90-day review	I want to notify the new hire of all of the requirements of the 90-day review	so they can begin to submit their evaluation in the system.
As an HR Rep	who has initiated a 90-day review	I want to notify the new hire of all of the requirements of the 90-day review	so they can begin to submit their evaluation in the system.
As an employee	who is under 90-day review	I want to create a log in for the HR review system	so that I can log in to submit my 90-day evaluation.
As an employee	who is under 90-day review	I want to log in to the system	so that I can view the requirements for my 90-day evaluation.
As an employee	who is under 90-day review	I want to submit the names of two peers I have worked with since being hired	so that they can contribute to my 90-day review.
As an employee	selected to peer review a new hire	I want to be notified when I have been selected to review a new hire after 90 days	so that I can log in to the system and submit my evaluation.

Figure 2.2 A Typical User Story and Its Lifecycle (Used with permission of Seilevel. *Source: Stowe, M. Going Agile: The Anatomy of a User Story,* at: https://seilevel.com/requirements/the-anatomy-of-a-user-story)

needed to meet their objectives. The following are those roles of the team that you commonly find in Scrum:

- **Scrum Master**—the person who serves as conductor and coach to help team members carry out their duties. Scrum masters are experts on Scrum, oversee the project throughout, and offer advice and direction. The Scrum master most often works on one project at a time, provides it their full attention, and focuses on improving the team's effectiveness.[5]
- **Analyst** roles work with the product owner and Scrum master to develop and refine the user stories that are submitted for development within a development sprint.
- **Architect** roles work on the design of the application architecture and design to meet the requirements described by the user stories. Design work is conducted in a design sprint, sometimes called *sprint zero*.
- **Designers** work on the aspects of the product that relate to user interfaces and user experience with the product. Essentially, designers are translators for the following aspects of the product[6]:
  - Translate users' desires and concerns **for product owners**.
  - Translate features **for users**—how the product will actually work and what it looks like.
  - Translate experiences and interfaces **for engineers**.
- **Engineer/Lead Engineer/Developers** work to build (code) the features for the applications based on user story requirements for each sprint.
- **Testers/Quality Assurance (QA) Leads** are those who work to determine if the application being delivered meets the acceptance criteria for the user stories and help to provide proof for the DoD for those user stories and, ultimately, the product.

As you'll see in Chapter 3, each of these roles require specialized application security training to help them to gain the skills they need for *ownership and responsibility* of security for their product.

2.4 Unwinding Sprint Loops

With the basic model and understanding of the roles people play within Scrum, let's now take a look at what happens inside each sprint as the cycle of development proceeds. Figure 2.3 expands on the steps inside a sprint loop.[7]

Under the paradigm of Building Security In, you can find opportunities for effective security controls throughout the product's lifecycle.

Beginning with **Requirements Refinement** for product backlog development, this is the opportunity to specify security functional and nonfunctional

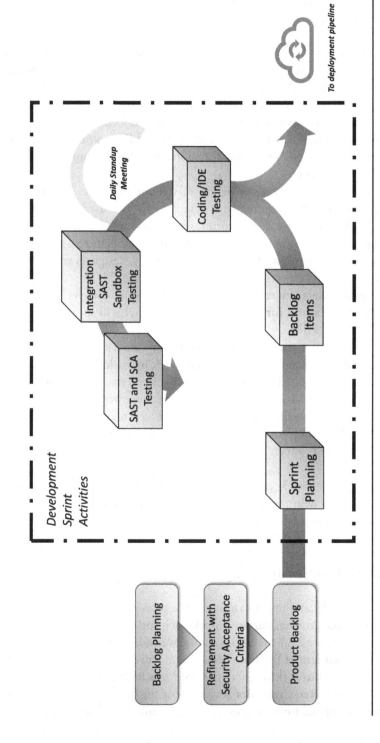

Figure 2.3 Expanded Activities Inside a Sprint

requirements (NFRs) as user stories or constraints on existing user stories in the form of acceptance criteria that drives the DoD. This approach forces everyone on the team to not only consider security, but also describe exactly how they plan to meet the control needs. This basic step will drive all follow-on activity to address security requirements and concerns head on through the analysis stage, the design stage, the development stage, the testing phases, and ultimately the acceptance phase prior to deployment of that release.

As constrained user stories enter a sprint, business systems analysts will refine these into specifications that are suitable for architecture and design work. As that work progresses and a final draft of a system design is available, the process of threat modeling and attack surface analysis will help to remove design defects that could lead to the most expensive and hardest to remediate vulnerabilities. Performing this work while remaining in the design sprint enables development teams to discover and fix the design or add controls that may be missed and serves as a phase-containment control to prevent defect creep. Threat modeling and other techniques for risk assessment are covered in Chapter 7.

Once an application design goes into the development activity, developers can use integrated development environment (IDE)-based security testing tools that can help them to identify and remove unit-based defects, such as use of insecure functions, failures to sanitize inputs, etc.

As the product comes together from the various developers working on units of it, and these units are collected for the application *build*, you find the first opportunity to perform static code analysis testing (SAST). Scanning can be set up within sandboxes in the development environment to help the team eliminate defects that can only be discovered in or after integration steps. Teams should be encouraged to use the IDE-based checker and the sandbox testing continuously as the application gains functionality. Open Source components and libraries used in the application can also be inspected for known vulnerabilities, using software composition analysis (SCA), and updated as needed with newer versions that patch those issues. Once static code scanning is complete, the latest, clean scan can be promoted as a policy gate scan as proof the application meets at least one DoD for security acceptance criteria.

As the methodology describes, this process repeats with each new sprint until a functionally complete, high-quality application is primed for release and deployment.

2.5 Development and Operations Teams Get Married

With the successful rise and proof of viability of Scrum to speed up software development, further changes made to speed up HOW software is deployed came on the scene with the marriage of development and operations.

In the "old" days, development teams would prepare change requests to throw the application over the wall for deployment and operations. These change requests would go through multiple levels of review and approvals, across multiple departments, to launch their software into production or make it available to the world. This process alone often took weeks or months.

Now, development teams and operations teams work together as partners for ongoing operations, enhancements, defect removal, and optimization of resources as they learn how their product operates in the real world.

As appsec professionals began integrating into planning for CI/CD, DevOps, and new models for data center operations, DevOps began to transform into what we'll call DevSecOps. It's also referred to as *Rugged DevOps, SecDevOps,* and just about any permutation you can think of.

Essentially, DevOps (and DevSecOps) strives to automate as much as possible, leaving time for people to perform quality-related activities that help to optimize how the application works.

From the time a version of software (a feature branch) is integrated and built (complied and packaged) for release, automation takes over. This automation is often governed by a **gatekeeper** function that orchestrates the process, runs suites of tests on the package, and will only allow the application to release if all the gate control requirements have been met. If a test reports an outcome that the gatekeeper's policy indicates a failure, the gatekeeper function can stop, or *break,* the build, necessitating attention and remediation from the product team. Testing automation might include using a broad set of testing

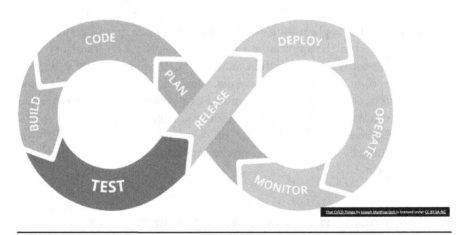

Figure 2.4   Agile and DevOps

(A description of Figure 2.4 can be found on page 18.)

DevSecOps cycle

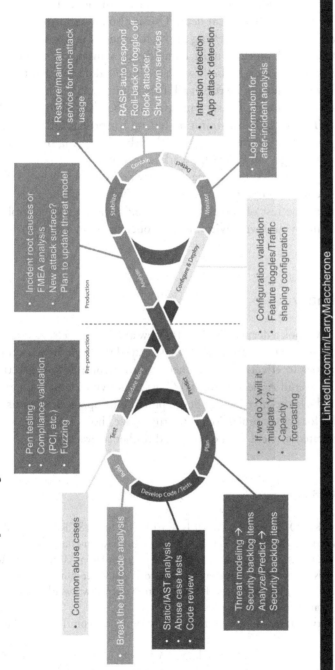

- Restore/maintain service for non-attack usage

- RASP auto respond
- Roll-back or toggle off
- Block attacker
- Shut down services

- Intrusion detection
- App attack detection

- Log information for after-incident analysis

- Incident root causes or FMEA analysis
- New attack surface?
- Plan to update threat model

- Configuration validation
- Feature toggles/Traffic shaping configuration

- Pen testing
- Compliance validation (PCI, etc.)
- Fuzzing

- If we do X will it mitigate Y?
- Capacity forecasting

- Common abuse cases

- Break the build code analysis

- Static/IAST analysis
- Abuse case tests
- Code review

- Threat modeling →
- Security backlog items
- Analyze/Predict →
- Security backlog items

Contain
Detect
Stabilize
Monitor
Analyze
Configure & Deploy
Production
Pre-production
Validate More
Predict
Test
Deploy
Plan
Develop Code / Tests

LinkedIn.com/in/LarryMaccherone

Figure 2.5 DevSecOps Cycle (Used with permission of L. Maccherone, Jr. *Source:* https://twitter.com/lmaccherone/status/843647960797888512)

(A description of Figure 2.5 can be found on page 18.)

tools that perform a wide variety of tests, such as functional tests, code quality and reliability tests, and technical debt. This is also an opportunity to include security-related tests, but that testing in the continuous integration/continuous deployment (CI/CD) pipeline must complete in a matter of seconds—or at worst, a few minutes—otherwise it won't be included as a gate for gatekeeper purposes, or worse, may not be run at all. Five minutes maximum is a good rule of thumb for the amount of extra time you may be allotted to test in the CI/CD pipeline. This specific constraint on testing is a primary driver of the shift left paradigm to adapt security controls within the SDLC. Figure 2.4 is a simple depiction on how Agile and DevOps work in unison[8]:

Figure 2.5 shows what the marriage of Dev and Ops teams looks like when comprehensive security controls transform DevOps into DevSecOps.[9]

Throughout the rest of the book, we'll look at how these controls can be implemented into your own environment to operate seamlessly with your existing practices.

2.6 Summary

In Chapter 2 we took a deeper dive into the new and improved software development world to see what's changed and what's stayed the same as we explore areas for opportunities to effectively implement security controls and practices. We examined the overall Agile/Scrum SDLC, roles, activities, and responsibilities. Next we saw how the marriage of development and operations teams provide opportunities for appsec professionals to "ruggedize" how applications are managed and operated to yield high quality and resilience every time.

References

1. Trapani, K. (2018, May 22). What Is AGILE? - What Is SCRUM? - Agile FAQ's. Retrieved from https://www.cprime.com/resources/what-is-agile-what-is-scrum/
2. Cohn, M. (n.d.). User Stories and User Story Examples by Mike Cohn. Retrieved from https://www.mountaingoatsoftware.com/agile/user-stories
3. Atlassian. (n.d.). User Stories. Retrieved from https://www.atlassian.com/agile/project-management/user-stories
4. User Story. (n.d.). Retrieved from https://milanote.com/templates/user-story-template
5. Understanding Scrum Methodology—A Guide. (2018, January 11). Retrieved from https://www.projectmanager.com/blog/scrum-methodology
6. Tan Yun (Tracy). (2018, July 3). Product Designers in Scrum Teams? Part 1. Retrieved from https://uxdesign.cc/design-process-in-a-scrum-team-part-1-d5b356559d0b

7. A Project Management Methodology for Agile Scrum Software Development. (2017, October 31). Retrieved from https://www.qat.com/project-management-methodology-agile-scrum/

8. Agile vs DevOps: Demystifying DevOps. (2012, August 3). Retrieved from http://www.agilebuddha.com/agile/demystifying-devops/

9. Maccherone, L. (2017, March 19). DevSecOps Cycle [Diagram]. Retrieved from https://twitter.com/lmaccherone/status/843647960797888512

Chapter 3

Learning Is FUNdamental!

As it turns out, throwing technology at defective software is likely the worst way to address appsec and ignores the basic tenet—*software security is a human factors issue, not a technical issue.* Tools are seductive with their *coolness* factor, ease of acquisition and use, and producing quick results that—in fact—tell you that you do have an issue with software security. Taking tools to the next step is where things quickly fall apart.

Suddenly, development teams are bombarded by reams of proof that their software is defective, and with finger-pointing from security teams, they're left in a state of upset and overall chaos. Furthermore, these development team members often don't understand what this proof is telling them and are completely unprepared to address these defects in any meaningful way.

Agile leads to an environment in which the incentives for developing new applications are found when the software is delivered quickly and as inexpensively as possible. Goodness or quality (or resilience or security) is not directly rewarded, and often the extra work required to address software goodness isn't given to development teams so they may address it.

Making matters worse, traditional college and private education that prepares programmers and IT roles for new technologies, new languages, and new platforms don't arm their students with the skills they need to meet the demands of organizations that require resilient, high-quality applications that can be constructed quickly at acceptable costs. Many development team members may enter the workforce never hearing the term *nonfunctional requirement.*

Each organization then finds they own the responsibility to break old bad habits, instill new good habits, and educate the workforce adequately to fill these gaps. To start the process, awareness of software security as an institutional issue is needed to set the stage for everything that follows. Awareness drives interest and curiosity and places people on the path to wanting to learn more. This awareness greases the skids that enable smooth engagement in software security education and ongoing involvement in appsec-related activities that "keep the drumbeat" alive throughout the year.

In this chapter, we're going to explore ways to bootstrap an awareness program that leads development team members into role-specific training to gain the right knowledge, skills, and abilities to succeed as defensive development teams.

3.1 Education Provides Context and Context Is Key

Without proper context, any mandates for high-quality, secure applications won't get communicated effectively to those who need to know. It's of little use to run around shouting that applications are vulnerable to cross-site scripting, SQL injection, buffer overruns, and so forth, if the people you're screaming at have little clue as to what they're hearing and even fewer skills or know-how to do something about it. To this end, although prevention is always better than remediating problems and rework, programmers are typically faced with learning their applications are insecure long after they've released them to production and to the malicious users who are pervasive throughout the Internet.

Software security is special-topic area for an overall practice of security education, training, and awareness (SETA) programs, in which various levels of awareness and training are needed to get through to the right people in their various roles within the software development lifecycle (SDLC). An effective program for building the right level of detail for each group of stakeholders uses a layering approach that builds on foundational concepts that are relevant and timely for each role in each phase.

3.2 Principles for Software Security Education

Here are some basic principles for consideration of what should be included or addressed when setting up an appsec awareness and education program:

- **Executive management sets the mandate.** With management mandates for secure application development that are widely communicated, you're given the appropriate *license to drive* a program from inception forward to continuous improvement. You'll need this executive support for

establishing a program, acquiring an adequate budget and staff, and keeping the program going in the face of setbacks or delays.

- **Awareness and training must be rooted in company goals, policies, and standards for software security.** Establishing, then using, docu-mented organizational goals, policies, and controls for secure application development as the basis for your awareness and training program creates a strong connection to developer actions that lead to compliance and "Defense in Depth" brought to life.
- **Learning media must be flexible and be tailored to the specific roles within your SDLC.** Not everyone can attend an in-person instructor-led course, so alternatives should be provided, such as computer-based train-ing, recorded live presentations, and so forth.
- **Learning should happen as close as possible to the point where it's needed.** A lengthy course that covers a laundry list of problems and solu-tions won't be useful when a specific issue crops up and the learner can't readily access whatever was mentioned related to the issue.
- **Learning and practicing go hand-in-hand.** As people personally experi-ence the "how to" of learning new skills, the better the questions they ask, and the quicker the knowledge becomes a regular practice.
- **Use examples from your own environment.** The best examples of secu-rity problems come from your applications. When people see issues with code and systems they're already familiar with, the consequences of exploit-ing the code's vulnerabilities hit close to home and become more real and less theoretical. Furthermore, demonstrating where these examples stray from internal standards for secure software helps people make the connec-tion between what they *should be* doing and what they've *been* doing.
- **Add learning milestones into your training and education program.** People are less motivated to learn and retain discrete topics and informa-tion if learning is treated as a "check box" activity. People want milestones in their training efforts that show progress and help them gain recogni-tion and demonstrate progress. As you prepare a learning curriculum for your various development roles, build in a way to recognize people as they successfully advance through the courses, and make sure everyone knows about it.
- **Make your program company culture relevant.** Find icons or internally well-known symbols in your organization that resonate with employees and incorporate them in your program or build your program around them.
- **BOLO.** Be On the Look Out for people who participate in your aware-ness and training program who seem more enthusiastic or engaged than others. These people are your candidates for becoming internal applica-tion security evangelists or application security champions. People love

thought leaders, especially when they're local, and you can harness their enthusiasm and interest to help you advance your program and your cause.

3.3 Getting People's Attention

When we're honest with ourselves, we know that software security is not the most exciting or engaging topic around. Apathy is rampant, and too many conflicting messages from prior attempts at software security awareness often cause people's eyes to glaze over, which leads to even further apathy and disconnection from the conversation.

Peter Sandman, who operates a risk communication practice, has identified a strategy for communication that's most appropriate for software security awareness, as well as other issues where apathy reigns but the hazards are serious (e.g., Radon poisoning, employee safety). The strategy, called *Precaution Advocacy*,[1] is geared toward motivating people by overcoming boredom with the topic. Precaution Advocacy is used on high-hazard, low-outrage situations in Sandman's Outrage Management Model. The advocacy approach arouses some healthy outrage and uses this attention to mobilize people to take, or demand, precautions.

Software security is a perfect issue for which it's difficult to overcome apathy and disinformation and motivate people to address the issues that only people can address and solve.

Precaution Advocacy suggests using four ways to getting people to listen—then learn:

1. **Learning without involvement**—The average television viewer pays little attention to the commercials, but nevertheless knows dozens of advertising jingles by heart. Repetition is the key here. Posters, closed-circuit TV segments, mouse pads, elevator wraps, etc., are some useful examples.
2. **Make your campaign interesting/entertaining**—If you can arouse people's interest or entertain them, you'll get their attention, and eventually you won't need so much repetition. It's best if you can make your awareness efforts impart interesting or entertaining messages often and liberally.
3. **Need to know**—Whetting people's appetite to learn encourages the learner to seek information, and it's easy to deliver information to people who are actively seeking it. Sandman[1] advises developers of awareness programs to focus less on delivering the information and more on motivating their audience to *want* to receive it. Empowering people helps you educate them. The more people understand that insecure software is a

software engineering, human-based problem (not a network security problem), the more they'll want to learn how best to prevent these problems. Making software security a personal issue for those who can effect improvements, then giving them the tools and skills to use, will make them more valuable team members and leads to better secured application software.

4. **Ammunition**—Psychologist Leon Festinger's "theory of cognitive dissonance"[2] argues that a great deal of learning is motivated by the search for ammunition to reduce the discomfort (or "dissonance") that people feel when they have done something or decided something they're not confident is wise. Overcoming cognitive dissonance is a vital step early in your awareness program, so people experience your information as supportive of their new behavior, rather than as hostile to their old behavior. People also need ammunition in their arguments with others. If others already believe that software security is a hazardous organizational-wide issue—with no cognitive dissonance—they won't need to pay so much attention to the arguments for doing it.

The last thing you want to do is frighten people or lead them to believe the sky is falling, but you do want to motivate them into changing their behavior in positive ways that improve software security and contribute to the organization's goals and success. As your program progresses, metrics can show how improvements in one area lead to reduced costs in other areas, simpler and less frequent bug fixing, improved pride of code ownership, and eventually best practices and reusable code components that are widely shared within the development community.

3.4 Awareness versus Education

Security awareness is the effective sharing of knowledge about potential and actual threats and an ability to anticipate and communicate what types of security threats developers face day after day. Security awareness and security training are designed to modify any employee behavior that endangers or threatens the security of the organization's information systems and data.

Beginning with an awareness campaign that's culturally sensitive, interesting, entertaining, memorable, and engaging gives you the head start you need to effect positive changes.

Awareness needs to reach everyone who touches software development in your organization—from requirements analysts to post-production support personnel. As you engage your workforce, be sure to keep the material fresh and in step with what's going on inside your organization. Provide employees with the information they need to engage in the follow-on steps of training and education and make those steps easy to complete and highly visible to anyone who's looking. Awareness needs to begin with an assumption of zero knowledge; don't assume your developers understand application security concepts, principles, and best practices—lay them out so they're easy to find and easy to assimilate. Define common terms (e.g., *threat, exploit, defect, vulnerability*) so everyone understands them the same way, reducing confusion.

As your awareness efforts take hold and people come to realize how their approach to software development affects the security of applications—and they begin asking the right questions—they'll be prepared to "do" something about security, and that's where education programs can take root. The BITS Software Security Framework[3] notes that, "[an] education and training program in a mature software security program represents the 'lubricant' to behavior change in developers and as a result, is an essential ingredient in the change process."

3.5 Moving into the Education Phase

While awareness efforts are never really considered "done," they can be progressively more detailed, preparing people for an education regimen that's tailored to their role.

People will naturally fall into one of several specific roles, and each role has specific needs for specific information. Don't invent new roles for development team members. Use the roles that are in place and hitch your wagon to the internal efforts to roll out and support Agile. All the roles on the Scrum team should be addressed with role-based appsec training:

- Architects and leads
  - Secure code starts with secure requirements and design.
  - Secure code does not equal secure applications.
  - Security is required through all phases of the process.
  - Gain skills in threat modeling and attack surface analysis.
- Developers/engineers/lead engineers
  - Match training to level of awareness and technologies used.
- Testers
  - Someone must verify the security of the end product.
  - Testers can vary in capability and may need hand-holding while they gain confidence in using security scanners and penetration testing tools.
- Information security personnel
  - They know security, they don't necessarily know about application development or application-specific security concerns.

- Management, including Scrum masters
  - Project and program management, line management and upper management.
  - Basics of application security risk assessments and risk management concepts and strategies
  - Need to understand specific risks so they budget the time and resources to address them.

Bundles or collections of courses can be assembled to address basic or baseline education, introductory education, intermediate and advanced or expert education. Figure 3.1 is one example of how courses might be bundled to address the various roles and the levels of learning.

3.6 Strategies for Rolling Out Training

Here are a few suggested approaches for rolling out your training program:

- Everybody gets everything.
  - Broadly deploy training level by level, team by team.
- Core training plus security specialists.
  - Specialists by functional groups, skills, or projects.
- Base training plus candidates for "software security champions or evangelists."
  - Less training for all, but a few go to people embedded in groups or projects.
  - "Train the Trainer" approach.
  - Multi-level support for developers with base training.
- Start slow.
  - Roll out to test group or organization.
  - Mix and match models and test.

Selecting one of these or a hybrid of strategies will depend on several factors that are specific to your organization. These factors include geographical dispersion to where your development teams are located, separation or concentration of groups who are responsible for mission-critical applications, existing infrastructures for educating employees, number of people available to conduct training, number of people needing training, etc. Learning programs come in all shapes and sizes. Some programs are suited to in-person training, others to online, computer-based training (CBT), or hybrids of the two. Gamification of learning has entered the field and includes the use of cyber ranges (discussed later) and computer-based learning delivered in a game-like environment.

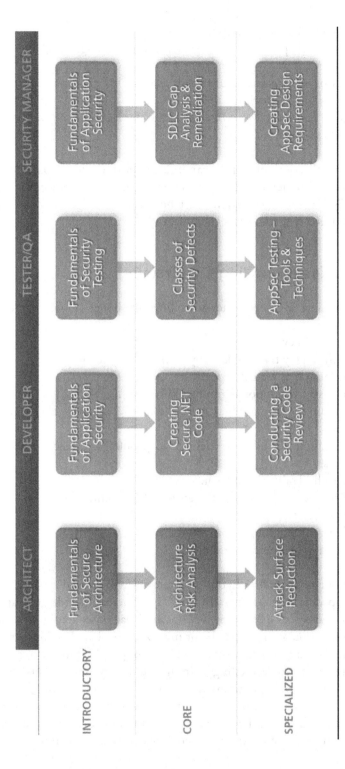

Figure 3.1 Bundles of Courses Stratified by Role in the SDLC (© Innovation Inc. Used with permission. *Source: Whitepaper: Rolling Out an Effective Application Security Training Program*[4])

3.7 Encouraging Training Engagement and Completion

Team members are under very tight time pressures to produce and have little time for "extra" training in software development security. Often push-back from team members and their management caused by assigning training to those who are already strapped for time may lead to training-related issues. At other times, there are managers of teams who stand out as excellent in how their teams complete the training in a reasonably quick period of time (3–4 months after it's assigned).

What some of these managers do is set aside some time in the Agile process itself to run a "training sprint," in which the 2–4 weeks of time allotted for a sprint is used for everyone to complete their training. Other managers set aside a work day and take their staff off-site for a training day, bring in lunch, and make it easier for team members to concentrate on training, and not the issue of the moment. You can even turn the effort into a type of friendly competition, using learning modules based on gamification of training.

3.8 Measuring Success

The OWASP OpenSAMM Maturity Model, discussed at length in Chapter 11— Metrics and Models for AppSec Maturity—describes a Level II of program maturity that supports a role-based education curriculum for development staff, under the Education and Guidance domain of OpenSAMM[5]:

> *Conduct security training for staff that highlights application security in the context of each role's job function. Generally, this can be accomplished via instructor-led training in 1–2 days or via computer-based training with modules taking about the same amount of time per person. For managers and requirements specifiers, course content should feature security requirements planning, vulnerability and incident management, threat modeling, and misuse/abuse case design. Tester and auditor training should focus on training staff to understand and more effectively analyze software for security-relevant issues. As such, it should feature techniques for code review, architecture and design analysis, runtime analysis, and effective security test planning. Expand technical training targeting developers and architects to include other relevant topics such as security design patterns, tool-specific training, threat modeling and software assessment techniques. To rollout such training, it is recommended to mandate annual security awareness training and periodic specialized topics training. Course should be available (either instructor-led or computer-based) as often as required based on head-count per role.*

At Level III maturity of Education and Guidance in OpenSAMM, the notion of certification for development roles appears. These types of certifications may be available internally though a custom-developed certification process, or in the marketplace through such programs as ISC²'s CSSLP[6] and/or SANS' GIAC[7] programs.

3.9 Keeping the Drumbeat Alive

Awareness efforts don't end as training efforts kick in—new people are hired all the time, team members change roles or teams, new technology is introduced, or strategic initiatives force all teams to re-examine how their applications are constructed, deployed, and operated.

Maintaining the appsec program on the radar screen with multiple, competing messages vying for the same attention is vital to help development teams to authentically take ownership and personal responsibility for their application's security.

Some ideas to keep the message alive include:

- **Brown bag** sessions on special topics of interest to a general audience of IT professionals. These topics should be at a sufficiently high level for engagement by those outside of software development: topics such as securing IoT for an organization that uses or produces them, trends in software development and software security, metrics from internal efforts, and invited guest speakers from the industry or the products you use to help with appsec. These brown bag sessions can be set up and conducted easily with desktop tools that are already in place (WebEx, Adobe Connect, etc.)
- **Newsletters** on specific topics in appsec for the development community are a great way to share information about new enhancements to appsec efforts, featured people (discussed later in this chapter), new tools coming on the scene, changes in security standards related to development, and even "Find the Bug" or "Find the Design Defect" challenges to help encourage applied application security.
- **Cyber ranges** are collections of resources that permit a participant to explore them on their own, use them in a competition, as a learning tool, or as a supplement to another form of training. A typical cyber range presents the user with a deliberately vulnerable application that "knows" when a vulnerability is exploited and awards points to the user to help them keep track of progress. Each user has their own version of the vulnerable application, so it differs from a hackathon in which participants attack or

defend a single system. You can run cyber range activities in an in-person setting, virtually for a fixed period of time, or some combination of the two. Cyber ranges are often available as a cloud offering, so you don't need to build the infrastructure to operate and manage it. You can find a list of cyber range resources at the end of this book.

- **Team or unit-based security working groups;** as the maturity of your program increases, and as team members take a deeper interest in their specific product or collection of products, you may be able to encourage the teams to form and operate a special-interest security working group for information and best practices sharing.

3.10 Create and Mature a Security Champion Network

Ideally, every Agile team will have its own security champion. These people act as liaisons to the appsec team in the security department, possess an intimate knowledge of the product they support, and demonstrate an interest in appsec. These champions will be the ones to help you promote and propagate changes or new activities that contribute to appsec.

Now and then, these people have questions of a nature that affect everyone who works on products in IT. Creating a community for your security champions is an important step you can take to maintain the program's growth and adoption. Collect this community together often (as reasonable) to help them to help themselves. Provide a forum or office hours for anyone who reaches out for help, and encourage your security champions to engage in advanced learning topics and help them if they elect to pursue certifications in IT security or appsec.

Aside from formal activities and media that you provide for your AppSec SETA Program, recognizing individuals for significant contributions or advancement of appsec efforts is another powerful tool for encouraging further engagement. Feature them and their effort in your newsletter or during a brown bag, and you'll gain a supporter of your program for life!

3.11 A Checklist for Establishing a Software Security Education, Training, and Awareness Program

The following checklist (see Table 3.1) is offered to help remind you of key principles and practices that we're certain will work. Consider these elements as you're formulating your overall customized appsec SETA program.

Table 3.1 Checklist for Education Program Success

✓	Requirement for Program Success
	Executive management establishes the mandate for software security and budgets the time, expense, and delegation of authority to improve software security.
	Company goals, policies, standards, and controls are in place for software security throughout the SDLC.
	Learning media is geared to your audience based on their availability, geographic dispersion, access to materials (intranet based vs. Internet based), language considerations, sensitivity of time zones where personnel are located.
	Reference tools are readily available to developers and are usable for just-in-time access for solving specific software security issues.
	Examples of high-quality and secure source code are available to show developers what needs to be accomplished and why.
	Code examples come from familiar internal sources.
	Courses are stratified by well-defined roles in the SDLC.
	Progress of courses and completion of course bundles include reward and recognition steps that further motivate learners.
	A metrics program has been established to show trends over time and help to identify components that are working as planned vs. those that need intervention or changes.
	Program maturity is measurable and is used consistently.

3.12 Summary

AppSec SETA Programs are an all-encompassing and difficult problem to address and solve and require dedication, effort, patience, and time to build an effective program. Awareness and education are vital for success and require a many-hats approach that includes psychology, creativity, engaging materials, formal structures for learners to navigate, and a solid rooting in how people learn and apply new skills in their jobs. As you apply these concepts and plan activities, events, and media for your program's ongoing communications, you will be well on the way to building the best program possible for yourself, your development teams, and your organization.

References

1. Snow, E. (n.d.). Motivating Attention: Why People Learn about Risk . . . or Anything Else (Peter Sandman article). SnowTao Editing Services. Retrieved from http://www.psandman.com/col/attention.htm
2. Cognitive Dissonance. (2007, February 5). Retrieved from https://www.simply psychology.org/cognitive-dissonance.html

3. BITS Software Security Framework. (2012). Retrieved from BITS website: http://www.bits.org/publications/security/BITSSoftwareAssurance0112.pdf
4. Security Innovation. (n.d.). Rolling Out An Effective Application Security Training Program. Retrieved from https://web.securityinnovation.com/rolling-out-an-effective-application-security-training-program/thank-you?submissionGuid=8c214b9b-e3fe-4bdb-8c86-c542d4cf1529
5. SAMM—Education & Guidance—2. (n.d.). Retrieved from https://www.owasp.org/index.php/SAMM_-_Education_&_Guidance_-_2
6. Software Security Certification | CSSLP—Certified Secure Software Lifecycle Professional | (ISC)^2. (n.d.). Retrieved from https://www.isc2.org/csslp/default.aspx
7. GIAC Security Certifications | Software Security Certifications. (n.d.). Retrieved from http://www.giac.org/certifications/software-security

Chapter 4

Product Backlog Development— Building Security In

Chapter 1 defines software resilience as the ability to *reduce the magnitude and/or duration of disruptive events*. The effectiveness of a resilient application or infrastructure software depends on its ability to *anticipate, absorb, adapt to, and/or recover rapidly* from a potentially disruptive event.

4.1 Chapter Overview

Chapter 4 shifts the focus to the beginning steps for product development, in which features are selected and written up as user stories and added to the product backlog. We'll first examine the classes and families for constraints on the product that need to be specified for purposes of resilience. We'll then look for ways to apply these constraints as acceptance criteria and Definition of Done attainment.

With a clear understanding of the nonfunctional requirements that constrain **how** a user story feature will be designed, developed, and tested, all of those on the Scrum team are working from the same playbook. By specifying these constraints up front, you've added key ingredients to the product development lifecycle that not only Build Security In, but enable various other desirable aspects, such as scalability, portability, reliability, and so on. Because one of the Agile goals for user stories is a change from *specifying what* needs to be present to *talking about* what needs to be present, and you can neatly include elements of performance, reliability, uptime, security, and so forth.

We'll examine 15 categories of nonfunctional requirements to help you to decide which characteristics are essential or desirable as you discuss user stories. From there we'll look at some concrete examples on how to use nonfunctional requirements (NFRs) as acceptance criteria and Definition of Done.

4.2 Functional versus Nonfunctional Requirements

Software is useful for what it does. People purchase software because it fulfills their need to perform some function. These functions (or features) can be as simple as allowing a user to type a letter or as complex as calculating the fuel consumption for a rocket trip to the moon. Functions and features are the reasons people purchase or pay for the development of software, and it's in these terms that people think about software.

What software is expected to "do" is described by a product owner as user stories, or *requirements* in the old vernacular. These requirements show up on the product backlog as they're collected and prioritized for development.

NFRs are the quality, security, and resiliency aspects of software that **only** show up in software specifications when they're deliberately added. These requirements come out when the major set of stakeholders who meet to discuss the planned product gets expanded beyond the people who will use it and includes the people who will:

- Operate it
- Maintain it
- Oversee the governance of the software development life cycle
- Serve as security professionals
- Represent legal and regulatory compliance groups who have a stake in assuring that the software is in compliance with local, state, and federal laws.

Although functional requirements state what the system *must do*, NFRs constrain how the system must *accomplish the what*.

In commercial software, you don't see these features or aspects of software advertised or even discussed on the package or in marketing literature for the software. Developers won't state that their program is more secure than their competitor's products, nor do they tell you much about the environment under which the software was developed. As purchasers of software, we don't tend to ask for the characteristics related to uptime, reliability, accuracy, or speed. We simply assume those characteristics are present. But providing these features is not free, cheap, or automatic. *Someone* has to build these in from the moment a user story is written!

Figure 4.1 illustrates what happens when requirements are ill-understood, poorly documented, or just assumed by development and support teams. Although this comic has been around for four decades, it's as relevant today as when it first came out.

4.3 Testing NFRs

Once software is developed, testing begins with making sure it meets its functional requirements: Does it perform what the user stories specify it needs to perform in the way they're specified to perform? Tests are developed for each use case or scenario described by the users, and if the software behaves as the acceptance criteria indicates it should, it's passed on for user acceptance testing.

Software testing that focuses only on functionality testing for user acceptance can uncover errors (defects or bugs or flaws) in how the software operates. If the system responds to input in the ways the users expect it to respond, it's stamped as ready to ship. If the system responds differently, the bugs are worked out in successive remediation and retesting sprints until it behaves as desired.

Testing for resilience in software is a whole other ballgame. Developers cannot test their own programs for anything more than determining whether a function works. Developers rarely test their programs for security flaws or stress the software to the point where its limitations are exposed or it fails to continue operating.

Resilience and security testing flip the problem of user acceptance testing on its head. Resilience tests not only verify that the functions designed to meet a nonfunctional requirement or service (e.g., security functions) operate as expected, it also validates that the implementation of those functions is not *flawed or haphazard.*

This kind of testing can only be performed effectively by experts and special-purpose tools. Over time, you can train QA testers on Scrum teams to run and consume the results of these tools to help enable the team's security self-sufficiency, or these tools can be automatically run earlier in a sprint to help prevent security defects from reaching QA testing.

Gaining confidence that a system *does not do what it's not supposed to do* is akin to proving a negative, and everyone knows that you can't prove a negative. What you can do, however, is subject a system to brutal types of testing, and with each resistance to an attack, gain increasing confidence that it was developed with a secure and resilience mindset from the very beginning.

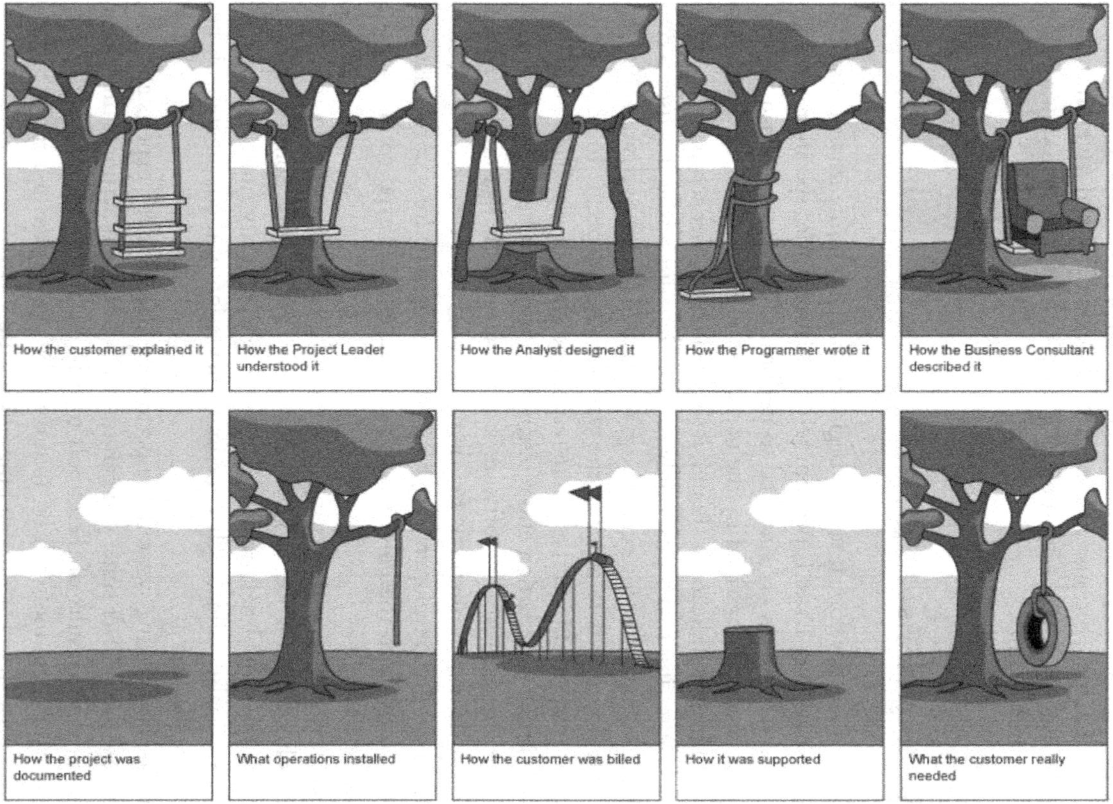

Figure 4.1 Software Development Pitfalls

4.4 Families of Nonfunctional Requirements

Resilient software demonstrates several characteristics that help to improve the lives of everyone who has a stake in or responsibility for developing it, maintaining it, supporting it, or using it as a foundation on which new features and functions are added. These characteristics fall into natural groups that address the following. They are listed alphabetically, not in order of importance:

- Availability
- Capacity
- Efficiency
- Extensibility
- Interoperability
- Manageability
- Maintainability
- Performance
- Portability
- Privacy
- Recoverability
- Reliability
- Scalability
- Security
- Serviceability

You may hear or see NFRs also called *design constraints, quality requirements,* or *"ilities,"* as referenced by the last part of their names. You'll also see that there is some overlap with NFRs: Some requirements address more than one aspect of quality and resilience requirements, and it's not important where this shows up, so long as it winds up as part of acceptance criteria or Definition of Done (or both), is accounted for in all development activities, and is tested to assure its presence and correct operation.

Here we'll examine these various areas and discuss some broad and some specific steps and practices to assure their inclusion in the final product.

4.4.1 Availability

Availability shows up again later as a goal of security, but other availability requirements address the specific needs of the users who access the system. These include maintenance time windows at which the software might be stopped for various reasons. To help users determine their availability requirements, experts recommend that you ask the following questions:

- What are your scheduled operations?
- What times of the day and what days of the week do you expect to be using the system or application?

The answers to these questions can help you identify times when the system or application must be available. Normally, responses coincide with users' regular working hours. For example, users may work with an application primarily from 8:00 a.m. to 5:00 p.m., Monday through Friday. However, some users want to be able to access the system for overtime or telecommuting work. Depending on the number of users who access the system during off-hours, you can choose to include those times in your normal operating hours. Alternatively, you can set up a procedure for users to request off-hours system availability at least three days in advance.

When external users or customers access a system, its operating hours are often extended well beyond normal business hours. This is especially true with online banking, Internet services, e-commerce systems, and other essential utilities such as electricity, water, and communications. Users of these systems usually demand availability 24 hours a day, 7 days a week, or as close to that as possible.

How often can you tolerate system outages during the times that you're using the system or application? Your goal is to understand the impact on users if the system becomes unavailable when it's scheduled to be available. For example, a user may be able to afford only two outages a month. This answer tells you whether you can ever schedule an outage during times when the system is committed to be available. You may want to do so for maintenance, upgrades, or other housekeeping purposes. For instance, a system that should be online 24 hours a day, 7 days a week may still require a scheduled downtime at midnight to perform full backups.

How long can an outage last, if one does occur? This question helps identify how long the user is willing to wait for the restoration of the system during an outage, or to what extent outages can be tolerated without severely affecting the business. For example, a user may say that any outage can last for up to a maximum of only three hours. Sometimes a user can tolerate longer outages if they are scheduled.[1]

Availability Levels and Measurements

Depending on the answers to the questions above, you should be able to specify which category of availability your users require, then proceed with design steps accordingly:

- High availability—The system or application is available during specified operating hours with no unplanned outages.
- Continuous operations—The system or application is available 24 hours a day, 7 days a week, with no scheduled outages.
- Continuous availability—The system or application is available 24 hours a day, 7 days a week, with no planned or unplanned outages.

The higher the availability requirements, the more costly the implementation will be to remove single points of failure and increase redundancy.

4.5 Capacity

When software designs call for the ability for support personnel to "set the knobs and dials" on a software configuration, instrumentation is the technique that's used to implement the requirement. With a well-instrumented program, variables affecting the runtime environment for the program are external to the program (not hard coded) and saved in an external file separate from the executing code. When changes are needed to add additional threads for processing, programmers need not become involved if system support personnel can simply edit a configuration file and restart the application. Capacity planning is made far simpler when runtime environments can be changed on the fly to accommodate changes in user traffic, changes in hardware, and other runtime-related considerations.

4.6 Efficiency

Efficiency refers to the degree that a system uses scarce computational resources, such as CPU cycles, memory, disk space, buffers, and communication channels.[2] Efficiency can be characterized using these dimensions:

- Capacity—Maximum number of users or transactions
- Degradation of service—The effects of a system with capacity of X transactions per time when the system receives X+1 transactions in the same period

NFRs for efficiency should describe what the system should do when its limits are reached or its use of resources becomes abnormal or out of pattern. Some examples here might be to alert an operator of a potential condition, limit further connections, throttle the application, or launch a new instance of the application.

4.7 Interoperability

Interoperability is the ability of a system to work with other systems or software from other developers without any special effort on the part of the user, the implementers, or the support personnel. Interoperability affects data exchanges at a number of levels: ability to communicate seamlessly with an external system or trading partner, semantic understanding of data that's communicated, and ability to work within a changing environment of hardware and support software. Interoperability can only be implemented when everyone involved in the development process adheres to common standards. Standards are needed for communication channels (e.g., TCP/IP), encryption of the channel when needed (e.g., SSL/TLS), databases (e.g., SQL), data definitions (e.g., using XML and standard Document Type Definitions, JSON objects), interfaces between common software functions and microservices (e.g., APIs), and so on. Interoperability requirements should dictate what standards must be applied to these elements and how the designers and developers can get their hands on them to enable compliant application software.

Interoperability is also concerned with use of internal standards and tools for development. When possible, new systems under development should take advantage of any existing standardized enterprise tools to implement specific features and functions—for example, single sign-on, cryptographic libraries, and common definitions of databases and data structures for internal uses.

4.8 Manageability

Manageability encompasses several other areas of NFRs but is focused on easing the ability for support personnel to manage the application. Manageability allows support personnel to move the application around available hardware as needed or run the software in a virtual machine, which means that developers should never tie the application to specific hardware or external non-supported software. Manageability features require designers and developers to build software as highly cohesive and loosely coupled. Coupling and cohesion are used as software quality metrics as defined by Stevens, Myers, and Constantine in an *IBM Systems Journal* article.[3]

4.8.1 Cohesion

Cohesion is increased when the responsibilities (methods) of a software module have many common aspects and are focused on a single subject and when these methods can be carried out across a variety of unrelated sets of data. Low cohesion can lead to the following problems:

- Increased difficulty in understanding the modules.
- Increased difficulty in maintaining a system, because logical changes in the domain may affect multiple modules, and because changes in one module may require changes in related modules.
- Increased difficulty in reusing a module, because most applications won't need the extraneous sets of operations that the module provides.

4.8.2 Coupling

Strong coupling happens when a dependent class contains a pointer directly to a concrete class that offers the required behavior (method). Loose coupling occurs when the dependent class contains a pointer only to an interface, which can then be implemented by one or many concrete classes. Loose coupling provides extensibility and manageability to designs. A new concrete class can easily be added later that implements the same interface without ever having to modify and recompile the dependent class. Strong coupling prevents this.

4.9 Maintainability

Software maintenance refers to the modification of a software application after delivery to correct faults, improve performance or other attributes, or adapt the product to a modified environment, including a DevSecOps environment.[4] Software maintenance is an expensive and time-consuming aspect of development. Software system maintenance costs are a substantial part of life-cycle costs and can cause other application development efforts to be stalled or postponed while developers spend inordinate amounts of time maintaining their own or other developers' code. Maintenance is made more difficult if the original developers leave the application behind with little or no documentation. Maintainability within the development process requires that the following questions be answered in the affirmative:

1. Can I find the code related to the problem or the requested change?
2. Can I understand the code?
3. Is it easy to change the code?
4. Can I quickly verify the changes—preferably in isolation?
5. Can I make the change with a low risk of breaking existing features?
6. If I do break something, is it easy to detect and diagnose the problem?

Maintenance is not an application-specific issue, but a software development environment issue: If there are few or no controls over what documentation is required, how documentation is obtained and disseminated, how the documentation itself is maintained, or if developers are given sufficient time to prepare original documentation, then maintainability of the application will suffer. It's not enough to include a requirement that "the software must be maintainable"; specific requirements to support maintainability with actionable events must be included in design documents. The Software Maintenance Maturity Model (SMmm)[5] was developed to address the assessment and improvement of the software maintenance function by proposing a maturity model for daily software maintenance activities. The SMmm addresses the unique activities of software maintenance while preserving a structure similar to that of the Software Engineering Institute's Capability Maturity Model integration (CMMi).

4.10 Performance

Performance (sometimes called *quality-of-service*) requirements generally address three areas:

- Speed of processing a transaction (e.g., response time)
- Volume of simultaneous transactions (e.g., the system must be able to handle at least 1,000 transactions per second)
- Number of simultaneous users (e.g., the system must be able to handle a minimum of 50 concurrent user sessions)

The end users of the system determine these requirements, and they must be clearly documented if there's to be any hope of meeting them.

4.11 Portability

Software is considered portable if the cost of porting it to a new platform is less than the cost of rewriting it from scratch. The lower the cost of porting software, relative to its implementation cost, the more portable it is. Porting is the process of adapting software so that an executable program can be created for a computing environment that is different from the one for which it was originally designed (e.g., different CPU, operating system, mobile device, or third-party library). The term is also used in a general way to refer to the changing of software/hardware to make them usable in different environments.

Portability is most possible when there is a generalized abstraction between the application logic and all system interfaces. When there's a requirement that the software under development be able to run on several different computing platforms—as is the case with web browsers, email clients, etc.—portability is a key issue for development cost reduction, and sufficient time must be allowed to determine the optimal languages and development environments needed to meet the requirement without the risk of developing differing versions of the same software for different environments, thus potentially increasing the costs of development and maintenance exponentially.

4.12 Privacy

Privacy is related to security in that many privacy controls are implemented as security controls, but privacy also includes non-security aspects of data collection and use. When designing a web-based application, it's tempting to collect whatever information is available to help with site and application statistics, but some of the practices used to collect this data could become a privacy concern. Misuse or overcollection of data should be prevented with specific requirements on what data to collect, how to store it, how long to retain it, what's permitted for use of the data, and letting data providers (users in most cases) determine if they want that data collected in the first place.

The U.S. Federal Trade Commission offers specific guidance on fair information practice principles that are related to four areas, along with other principles for collecting information from children[6]:

1. Notice/Awareness
2. Choice/Consent
3. Access/Participation
4. Integrity/Security

1. Notice/Awareness—In general, a website should tell the user how it collects and handles user information. The notice should be conspicuous, and the privacy policy should state clearly what information the site collects, how it collects it (e.g., forms, cookies), and how it uses it (e.g., Is information sold to market research firms? Available to meta-search engines?). Also, the policy should state how the site provides the other "fair practices": choice, access, and security.

2. Choice/Consent—Websites must give consumers control over how their personally identifying information is used. This includes marketing directly to the consumer, activities such as "purchase circles," and selling information to

external companies such as market research firms. The primary problems found here involve collecting information for one purpose and using it for another.

3. Access/Participation—Perhaps the most controversial of the fair practices, users should be able to review, correct, and in some cases delete personally identifying information on a particular website. Inaccurate information or information used out of context can ruin a person's life or reputation.

4. Security/Integrity—Websites must do more than reassure users that their information is secure with a "feel-good" policy statement. The site must implement policies, procedures, and tools that will prevent anything from unauthorized access to personal information to hostile attacks against the site. Of biggest concern is the loss of financial information such as credit card numbers, bank account numbers, etc. You'll find a separate section on security requirements later in this chapter.

In 2018, the European Union (EU) General Data Protection Regulation (GDPR) took effect as a legal framework that sets guidelines for the collection and processing of personal information from individuals who live in the EU. Since the Regulation applies regardless of where websites are based, compliance is mandated by all sites that attract European visitors, even if they don't specifically market goods or services to EU residents. The GDPR mandates that EU visitors be given a number of data disclosures. The site must also take steps to facilitate such EU consumer rights as timely notification in the event of personal data being breached. Adopted in April, 2016, the Regulation came into full effect in May, 2018, after a two-year transition period.[7]

Depending on the market for your product, you may need to pay much closer attention to privacy than ever before.

4.13 Recoverability

Recoverability is related to reliability and availability but is extended to include requirements on how quickly the application must be restored in the event of a disaster, unexpected outage, or failure of a dependent system or service. Recoverability requires answers to the following questions:

- How important is the system or application to your company? Is it mission critical, is it used by all employees during normal working hours (e.g., email systems)? Is its use limited to a subset of employees who require only periodic access?
- How fast must you be able to restore full or partial service (in minutes, hours, days, weeks)? Will extended downtime of the application cause

employees to stay home until it's restored? How much money on average will your company lose if the application cannot be accessed by customers or trading partners?

Business impact analysis (BIA) can help to tease out these details, and when the process is applied across the entire population of business units, applications, and systems, it helps a company determine the overall priority for restoring services to implement the company's business continuity plan.

Table 4.1 outlines one possible set of application criticality levels that can be used for planning, along with some possible strategies for recovering applications for these levels.

Table 4.1 Levels of Software Criticality[8]

Criticality Level	Recovery Objective	Possible Recovery Method
Level 1: The business process must be available during all business hours.	<2 hours	Data replication
Level 2: The business function can survive without normal business processes for a limited amount of time.	2 hours to 24 hours	Data shadowing
Level 3: The business function can survive for 2 to 3 days with a data loss of 1 day.	24 to 72 hours	Media recovery at an offsite facility
Level 4: The business unit can survive without the business function for an extended period of time.	72 hours plus	Low priority for media recovery/rebuild infrastructure/relocate operations to a new facility

4.14 Reliability

Reliability requirements are an entire field of study all on their own, but reliability generally refers to a system's ability to continue operating in the face of hostile or accidental impacts to related or dependent systems. Reliability is far more critical when lives are at stake (e.g., aircraft life-support software, autonomous vehicles, medical devices) than they might be for business software. However, users and analysts need to consider and document how they expect the software to behave when conditions change. Reliability may be defined in several ways:

- The capacity of a device or system to perform as designed
- The resistance to failure of a device or system
- The ability of a device or system to perform a required function under stated conditions for a specified period of time

- The probability that a functional unit will perform its required function for a specified interval under stated conditions
- The ability of something to "fail well" (i.e., fail without catastrophic consequences)

Even the best software development process results in some software faults that are nearly undetectable until the software is tested.

4.15 Scalability

Scalability is the ability of a system to grow in its capacity to meet the rising demand for its services offered and is related to capacity NFRs.[9] System scalability criteria might include the ability to accommodate increasing number of:

- Users
- Transactions per second
- Number of database commands that can run and provide results simultaneously

The idea behind supporting scalable software is to force designers and developers to create functions that *don't prevent* the software from scaling. Practices that might prevent the software from scaling include hard coding of usage variables into the program that require manual modification and recompilation for them to take effect. A better choice is to include these constraints in an editable configuration file so that developers do not need to get involved every time their program is moved to a new operating environment.

4.16 Security

Security NFRs are needed to preserve the goals of confidentiality, integrity, and availability. Confidentiality is concerned with keeping data secure from those who lack "need to know." This is sometimes referred to as the *principle of least privilege*. Confidentiality is intended primarily to assure that no unauthorized access is permitted and that accidental disclosure is not possible. Common signs of confidentiality controls are user ID and password entry prior to accessing data or resources.

Integrity is concerned with keeping data pure and trustworthy by protecting system data from intentional or accidental changes. Integrity NFRs have three goals:

- Prevent unauthorized users from making modifications to data or programs.
- Prevent authorized users from making improper or unauthorized modifications.
- Maintain internal and external consistency of data and programs.

Availability is concerned with keeping data and resources available for authorized use when they're needed. Two common elements of availability as a security control are usually addressed:

- Denial of service due to intentional attacks or unintentional denial because of undiscovered flaws in implementation (e.g., buffer overflow conditions)
- Loss of information system capabilities caused by natural disasters (e.g., fires, floods, storms, or earthquakes) or human actions (e.g., bombs or strikes)

Here is just a beginning few security objectives that are needed for software that's expected to be secure and resilient:

- Ensure that users and client applications are identified and that their identities are properly verified.
- Ensure that all actions that access or modify data are logged and tracked.
- Ensure that internal users and client applications can only access data and services for which they have been properly authorized.
- Detect attempted intrusions by unauthorized persons and client applications.
- Ensure that unauthorized malicious programs (e.g., viruses) do not infect the application or component.
- Ensure that communications and data are not intentionally corrupted.
- Ensure that parties to interactions with the application or component cannot later repudiate (deny participation in) those interactions.
- Ensure that confidential communications and data are kept private.
- Enable security personnel to audit the status and usage of the security mechanisms.
- Ensure that applications can survive an attack or fail securely.
- Ensure that system maintenance does not unintentionally disrupt the security mechanisms of the application, component, or system.[10]

To assure that these objectives will be met, you'll need to document specific and detailed security requirements for the following:

- Identification requirements
- Authentication requirements
- Authorization requirements
- Immunity requirements
- Integrity requirements
- Intrusion-detection requirements
- Nonrepudiation requirements
- Privacy requirements
- Security auditing requirements
- Survivability requirements
- System maintenance security requirements[11]

Clearly, there are hundreds of individual requirements or constraints that may be needed to support these categories, and we'll look at some examples later in this chapter. You can also find a collection of 93 pre-written security-related functional and nonfunctional requirements in *Secure and Resilient Software: Requirements, Test Cases, and Testing Methods.*[12] You can easily recast these as user stories, acceptance criteria, or DoD constraints. As you collect and document these, they're easily and readily reusable on subsequent development projects.

4.17 Serviceability/Supportability

Serviceability and supportability refer to the ability of application support personnel to install, configure, and monitor computer software, identify exceptions or faults, debug or isolate faults to perform root-cause analysis, and provide hardware or software maintenance to aid in solving a problem and restoring the software to service. Incorporating serviceability NFRs results in more efficient software maintenance processes and reduces operational costs while maintaining business continuity.

Some examples of requirements that facilitate serviceability and supportability include:

- Help desk notification of exceptional events
- Network monitoring
- Standardized documentation tools and processes
- Event logging
- Logging of program state (e.g., execution path and/or local and global variables)
- Procedure entry and exit with input and return variable states

- Graceful degradation, whereby the software is designed to allow recovery from exceptional events without intervention by support staff
- Hardware replacement or upgrade planning, whereby the product is designed to allow efficient hardware upgrades with minimal computer system downtime (e.g., hot swaps)

4.18 Characteristics of Good Requirements

As you're collecting and documenting NFRs to use as acceptance criteria, it's not important that every category of NFR have at least one or more specific representation. As you're seeing, the overlap of coverage by the NFRs is there as food for thought—requirements are not generally organized by which NFRs they meet. What is important is that your analysis is thorough and that all aspects of software resilience are considered. What's also important is that these requirements be documented to meet the criteria of a "good" requirement statement. Table 4.2 lists some of the attributes for good requirements and may be used to help refine them as you document them.[13]

Another approach to determine if NFRs meet the characteristics of goodness is to use the SMART mnemonic for their development:

- Specific—Is it without ambiguity, using consistent terminology, simple, and at the appropriate level of detail?
- Measurable—Can you verify that this requirement has been met? What tests must be performed, or what criteria must be met to verify that the requirement is met?
- Attainable—Is it technically feasible? What is your professional judgment of the technical "do-ability" of the requirement?
- Realistic—Do you have the right resources? Is the right staff available? Do they have the right skills? Do you have enough time?
- Traceable—Is it linked from its conception through its specification to its subsequent design, implementation, and test?[14]

4.19 Eliciting Nonfunctional Requirements

Nonfunctional requirements are dictated by the operating environment and its support personnel, users, competitive product analysis (if any); industry, government, or corporate policies; and the internal software development process governance professionals. Regardless of what software development methodology the company has adopted, requirements-gathering sessions should include

Table 4.2 Characteristics of Good Requirements

Characteristic	Explanation
Cohesive	The requirement addresses one and only one thing.
Complete	The requirement is fully stated in one place with no missing information.
Consistent	The requirement does not contradict any other requirement and is fully consistent with all authoritative external documentation.
Correct	The requirement meets all or part of a business or resilience need as authoritatively stated by stakeholders.
Current	The requirement has not been made obsolete by the passage of time.
Externally observable	The requirement specifies a characteristic of the product that is externally observable or experienced by the user.
Feasible	The requirement can be implemented within the constraints of the project.
Unambiguous	The requirement is stated concisely, without unnecessary technical jargon, acronyms, or other esoteric terms or concepts. The requirement statement expresses objective fact, not subjective opinion. It is subject to one and only one interpretation. Vague subjects, adjectives, prepositions, verbs, and subjective phrases are avoided. Negative statements and compound statements are not used.
Mandatory	The requirement represents a stakeholder-defined characteristic or constraint.
Verifiable	Implementation of the requirement can be determined through one of four possible methods: inspection, analysis, demonstration, or test. If testing is the method needed for verifiability, the documentation should contain a section on how a tester might go about testing for it and what results would be considered passing.

representatives from the normal software stakeholder community (the "usual suspects"), along with the business users and a technical development leader. Make sure there's sufficient time in the session to focus on nonfunctional requirements so that everyone understands why they're necessary and the business sponsors are willing to pay for them. This might lead to some back-and-forth tension, but it's an essential activity in development projects to eliminate surprises later. When controls are first imposed on people by those who have the authority to impose them, resistance is often the first response. As people begin to understand that their desires for an unfettered application flies in the face of reality, they usually come around and eventually begin advocating for software development practices that result in resilient applications, and the cycle continues.

Agile has most certainly changed how we used to express requirements in formal documents like Business Requirements Documentation (BRDs) and

Master Requirements Documentation (MRDs). Today, there's no sign of those kinds of documents, and so appsec teams must adapt.

While some Agile and Scrum purists prefer user stories for every kind of function the product must perform, including performance needs, capacity needs, etc., it turns out it's more practical to use these needs as constraints expressed as acceptance criteria for each user story. The approach honors the principle of Building Security In and it uses the Agile methodology itself for built-in, focused attention to quality and resilience for all the "ilities."

4.20 NFRs as Acceptance Criteria and Definition of Done

Acceptance criteria are the conditions of satisfaction that must be met for that item to be accepted. User stories often have several elements for acceptance criteria. An example of using acceptance criteria for NFRs:

User Story: As a financial analyst, I want to see the monthly transactions for my customers so that I can advise them on their financial health.

Acceptance criteria:

- System displays all transactions meeting the search parameters within 10 seconds of receiving the request.
- Transactions for customers tagged as confidential are only displayed to users with Level 2 security.

Some NFRs are applicable across the entire product, so you may choose to express those requirements in the team's Definition of Done for the product.

In this case, the Definition of Done is a consistent set of acceptance criteria that applies to all backlog items. It's a comprehensive checklist indicating what "Done" looks like both in terms of functionality and NFR quality attributes, including accessibility, performance, security, or usability.[15]

In *Secure and Resilient Software—Secure and Resilient Software: Requirements, Test Cases, and Testing Methods*[11]—the 93 pre-written requirements are cast in the *old-fashioned way* for the families of security functional and nonfunctional requirements. You can reuse these documented requirements (available as MS Word documents) as a set of pre-written acceptance criteria and DoD constraints. This will spare you from the time it takes to develop solid criteria for reuse across teams and products. Furthermore, you can use the test cases tied to each requirement to help QA testers in their efforts to verify acceptance criteria and DoD needs.

4.21 Summary

There's no question that deriving nonfunctional requirements in software development projects is a daunting and enormous task that requires dozens of labor-hours from a cross-section of people who have a stake in the computing environment. Although some people may consider the exercise of gathering NFRs as wasted time, the fact remains that ignoring NFRs or making a conscious decision to eliminate them from software designs only kicks the problem down the road, where maintenance, support, and operational costs quickly negate any benefits the software was planned to provide.

In this chapter we discussed 15 categories of NFRs that can serve as food for thought during the requirements-gathering and analysis phases. We covered some of the best practices for eliciting requirements and found some effective ways of elaborating them for use in the earliest stages of the project. The influence of NFRs on the entire SDLC cannot be overemphasized.

References

1. Harris Kern Enterprise Computing Institute. (n.d.). Managing User Service Level Expectations. Retrieved from http://www.harriskern.com/wp-content/uploads/2012/05/Managing-User-Service-Level-Expectations.pdf
2. Chung, L. (2006). Non-functional Requirements. Retrieved from http://www.utdallas.edu/~chung/RE/2.9NFR.pdf
3. Stevens, W., Myers, G., and Constantine, L. (1974). Structured Design. *IBM Systems Journal,* 13(2), 115–139.
4. Canfora, G. and Cimitile, A. (2000, November 29). *Software Maintenance.* Retrieved from https://pdfs.semanticscholar.org/4393/e3d118269f374df7f9828a7be034b645336b.pdf
5. April, A., Hayes, J. H., Abran, A., and Dumke, R. (2005, May). Software Maintenance Maturity Model (SMmm): The Software Maintenance Process Model. *Journal of Software Maintenance and Evolution: Research and Practice,* 17(3), 197–223. Retrieved from https://onlinelibrary.wiley.com/doi/abs/10.1002/smr.311
6. Federal Trade Commission. (n.d.). Retrieved from http://www.ftc.gov/reports/privacy3/fairinfo.shtm
7. General Data Protection Regulation (GDPR). (2016, November 25). Retrieved from https://www.investopedia.com/terms/g/general-data-protection-regulation-gdpr.asp
8. GIAC Forensics, Management, Information, IT Security Certifications. (n.d.). Retrieved from http://www.giac.org/resources/whitepaper/planning/122.php
9. Weinstock, C. B. and Goodenough, J. B. (2006, March). On System Scalability. Retrieved from https://pdfs.semanticscholar.org/00d3/17340a32f2dace4686b7b988761abc1bfd43.pdf

10. Firesmith, D. G. Engineering Security Requirements. Retrieved from http://www.jot.fm/issues/issue_2003_01/column6/

11. Merkow, M. and Ragahvan, L. (2011). *Secure and Resilient Software: Requirements, Test Cases, and Testing Methods.* 1st Ed. Auerbach Publications.

12. Ibid.

13. Fricker, S. A. and Schneider, K. (2015). *Requirements Engineering: Foundation for Software Quality.* Retrieved from https://books.google.com/books?id=KLln BwAAQBAJ

14. Oracle. (n.d.). Understanding Requirements. Retrieved from https://docs.oracle.com/cd/E13214_01/wli/docs92/bestpract/requirementsappendix.html

15. Saboe, D. (2019, April 10). Non-Functional Requirements in Agile. Retrieved from https://masteringbusinessanalysis.com/lightning-cast-non-functional-require ments-in-agile/

Chapter 5

Secure Design Considerations

Up to this point we have examined the steps to enhance the Scrum process with security activities that lead to secure and resilient application software. We have seen how new activities must make their way into existing processes to account for deliberate actions that lead to high software quality. In Chapter 5 we'll overlay basic principles and practices atop the acceptance criteria and Definition of Done from Chapter 4.

5.1 Chapter Overview

To aid in designing new high-quality software, application security and resilience principles and best practices are essential for developing solutions, because there are no universal recipes for sure-fire secure and resilient software development. Every environment is unique, with unique practices and processes. Principles help designers and developers to "do the right things," even when they have incomplete or contradictory information. This chapter provides details on some of these critical concepts related to web application security and distills them into 10 principles and practices (outlined below) that you can use to help design high-quality systems and to educate others in their pursuit of secure and resilient application software.

5.2 Essential Concepts

At one time, in the Jurassic period of internal client–server applications and glass-house mainframe applications, administrators of networks and servers could rely on network security controls to protect users and devices from malicious or unwanted communications. Entire network architectures consisting of firewalls, routers, and intrusion detection and prevention devices limited outside traffic to only supported protocols and services, while all others were blocked or prevented from entering the network. As history clearly shows us now, "The Internet Changes Everything!"

5.3 The Security Perimeter

To help people better understand the issues of secure software development, we adopt some of the concepts of security from the real world. One such concept is the *security perimeter or trust boundary*. A simple definition of the security perimeter is *the border between the assets we want to protect and the outside world*. It is where we deploy our first line of defense.

Physical security controls are meant to prevent and/or deter attackers from accessing a private property without authorization. We can consider implementing several measures:

- A locked gate
- A fence or high wall around the property
- A security guard at the entrance
- Security cameras
- Automated security monitoring and alarm systems

We see the security perimeter concept in our everyday lives—an airport is one good example. The U.S. Transportation Security Administration (TSA) creates a security perimeter with physical barriers and scans every person who crosses the security perimeter to enter into what we call a "secure zone" or "sterile area." The TSA not only scans people, it also scans the objects they carry (both hand and checked-in baggage) that wind up in the secure zone.

This concept of a trusted and secured zone and a security check for whatever enters that zone is applicable to software and networks of today's businesses. However, it is becoming increasingly difficult to define the ever-expanding and ambiguous nature of the security perimeter of an organization because of several factors:

- Cloud computing in all forms
- Extranets and virtual private networks
- Globally telecommuting employees
- Mobile technologies
- Opening up of back-office services to public users and automation

As the borders of enterprise network continue to blur, it is difficult to rely on traditional security mechanisms to secure assets. The trust models and the security controls implemented to monitor and validate them are completely different and very sophisticated. Years ago, we believed and behaved as if anything behind an enterprise's firewalls was secure and trusted. We were wrong then and we're wrong now . . .

Let's look at an example of a typical three-tier web application. We can define a security perimeter around the application only. The application has control over the elements that are inside the application perimeter:

- Web server(s)
- Application server(s)
- Database server(s)

The application has no control over the elements outside the application perimeter:

- Web browsers
- Other applications
- External databases

The web application is responsible for ensuring that the proper controls are in place to protect itself from malicious activity, and it is the last line of defense.

User input coming from the user's browser is not under any control by the application. Data emanating from other applications or external databases is also beyond the control of the application. In many cases, the application will have to verify and appropriately encode the data coming from its own trusted database before it presents it to an end user. The bottom line is that the application must assume that nothing outside its security perimeter or trust boundary can be trusted. We'll discuss this in more detail relative to how static-code scanners operate in Chapter 8.

Enterprises today cannot afford to deploy IT resources like candy shells or eggs—hard on the outside but soft and mushy on the inside. There are several zones of trust and security within computer networks, operating systems, and applications. The principle of *Defense in Depth* plays a significant role in securing them appropriately, as we'll discover later in this chapter.

5.4 Attack Surface

Attack surface is a highly useful concept to identify, assess, and mitigate risks to today's software systems. A simple definition of an attack surface is *all possible entry points that an attacker can use to attack the application or system under consideration.* It is the area within the network or application that is visible to an attacker and may potentially be attacked. In a typical environment, open sockets or ports, web services API entry points, or any service that is inside a firewall perimeter but is made available externally constitutes the attack surface. Even a human who is susceptible to a social engineering attack is considered part of the attack surface. The largest contributors to the attack surface, however, are web applications. While typical services such as telnet and FTP may be effectively blocked by a firewall, web applications running on Port 80 (HTTP) and Port 443 (HTTPS) are open to the Internet and to all of those people wishing to exploit problems they may find in them. These web applications are the final frontier for hackers.

In the case of a web application, the attack surface is defined by:

- All the web pages the attacker can access, either directly or forcibly
- Every point at which the attacker can interact with the application (all input fields, hidden fields, cookies, or URL variables)
- Every function provided by the application

The exact attack surface depends on who the attacker is (internal versus external presence):

- Malicious application users may gain access to unauthorized functionalities.
- External attackers usually have limited access (unauthenticated areas of the application).

5.4.1 Mapping the Attack Surface

The attack surface is usually larger than a typical application developer or software architect imagines. It can be exhaustively identified using attack surfacing mapping techniques. In the case of a web application, the following techniques are often used:

- Crawl every page of the application (using an automated tool).
- Identify all the available functionalities:
  - Follow every link.
  - Fill every form with valid/invalid data and submit.
- Look for the points at which the user can supply information to the application:
  - GET requests with query strings parameters
  - POST requests generated by forms
  - HTTP headers
  - Cookies
  - Hidden parameters

Research on attack surfaces in general and ways to quantify and reduce them is increasing. An *attack surface metric* was proposed by researchers at Carnegie Mellon University during research sponsored by the U.S. Army Research office to measure the attack surface.[1]

5.4.2 Side Channel Attacks

Sometimes attackers target the implementation (typically in cryptosystems) rather than the actual theoretical weakness in a system. These attacks, called *side channel attacks*, are critical areas for designers and developers who are designing and deploying secure hardware and software systems.

A simple example of a side channel attack is the *timing attack*. A "smart card" that is used for cryptographic purposes has embedded integrated circuits that can store and process data. The cryptographic keys are stored securely in the card and never physically leave the card. Some of them even have a physical booby trap that will zero the memory if the smart card circuitry is physically tampered with to access the keys or force it into an insecure state. On the surface, this seems to be a highly resistant and secure system to store keys and perform cryptography operations. However, by watching (monitoring) the data movement in and out of the smart card, some attackers have been able to reconstruct the key that is securely stored in the smart card.

Here is a simple but odd, real-world example to help you understand this type of timing attack. If a person is asked to pick and retrieve different items, one at a time, at a supermarket, it's possible to measure the time it takes for each item to be brought back to determine the relative positions of the different areas of the store and to guess the location of other related items in the store. Through iterative monitoring and analysis, a side channel attack can force information to "leak," increasing the likelihood of success with subsequent attacks.

With an understanding of the security perimeter and attack surface, we can begin to look at security and resilience principles and practices that can help minimize problems related to the frenzy of work that goes on to extend and enrich the experience of their Internet presence.

5.5 Application Security and Resilience Principles

The principles here include desirable application properties, behaviors, designs, and implementation guidance and practices that attempt to reduce the likelihood of threat realization and impact, should that threat be realized. These principles are language independent and architecturally neutral primitives that can be leveraged within most software development methodologies to design and construct applications.[2] Principles are important because they help us make decisions in new situations using the same basic ideas. By considering each of these principles, we can derive security and resilience attributes that are needed, make architecture and implementation decisions, and identify possible weaknesses in systems.

What is important to remember is that, to be useful, the principles must be evaluated, interpreted, and applied to address a *specific problem*. Following are 10 principles and best practices, adapted from the Open Web Application Security Project (OWASP):

1. Apply *defense in depth*.
2. Use a positive security model.
3. Fail securely.
4. Run with *least privilege*.
5. Avoid *security by obscurity*.
6. Keep security simple.
7. Detect intrusions.
8. Don't trust infrastructure.
9. Don't trust services.
10. Establish secure defaults.[3]

Although these principles can serve as general guidelines, simply telling a software developer that their software must "fail securely" or that they should apply "defense in depth" does not mean very much and won't produce the desired results.

5.5.1 Practice 1: Apply Defense in Depth

The principle of *defense in depth* emphasizes that security is increased markedly when it is implemented as a series of overlapping layers of controls and countermeasures that provide three elements needed to secure assets: prevention, detection, and response.

Defense in depth, both as a military concept as well as implementation in software and hardware, dictates that security mechanisms be layered in a manner such that the weaknesses of one mechanism are countered by the strengths of two or more other mechanisms.

Think of a vault as an example. A bank or jewelry store would never entrust its assets to an unguarded safe alone. Most often, access to the safe requires passing through layers of protection that may include human guards, locked doors with special access controls (biometrics such as fingerprints or retinal scans, electronic keys, etc.), or two people working in concert to gain access (dual control). Furthermore, the room where the safe is located may be monitored by closed-circuit television, motion sensors, and alarm systems that can quickly detect unusual activity and respond with the appropriate actions (lock the doors, notify the police, or fill the room with tear gas).

In the software world, defense in depth dictates that you should layer security devices in series that protect, detect, and respond to likely attacks on the systems. Figure 5.1 illustrates the concept of defense in depth.[4] Note the groupings and the layering of adjacent controls. The security of each of these mechanisms must be thoroughly tested before deployment to help gain the needed confidence that the integrated system is suitable for normal operations. After all, a chain is only as good as its weakest link.

For example, it's a terrible idea to rely solely on a firewall to provide security for an internal-use-only application, because firewalls can be circumvented by a determined and skilled attacker. Other security mechanisms should be added to complement the protection that a firewall affords (intrusion-detection devices, security awareness training for personnel, etc.) to address different attack vectors, including the human factor.

The principle of defense in depth does not relate to a particular control or subset of controls. It is a design principle to guide the selection of controls for an application to ensure its resilience against different forms of attack and to reduce the probability of a single point of failure in the security of the system.

5.5.2 Practice 2: Use a Positive Security Model

The positive security model that is often called "whitelisting" defines what is allowable and rejects everything that fails to meet the criteria. This positive model should be contrasted with a "negative" (or "blacklist") security model, which defines what is disallowed, while implicitly allowing everything else.

One of the more common mistakes in application software development is the urge to "enumerate badness," or begin using a blacklist. Like antivirus (AV)

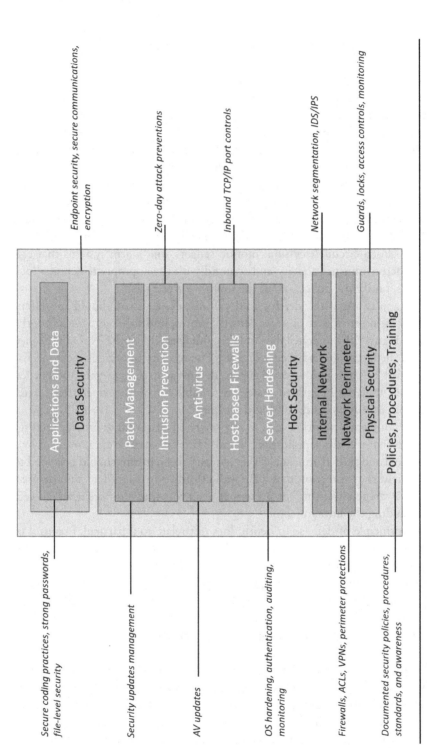

Secure coding practices, strong passwords,
file-level security

Security updates management

AV updates

OS hardening, authentication, auditing,
monitoring

Firewalls, ACLs, VPNs, perimeter protections

Documented security policies, procedures,
standards, and awareness

Endpoint security, secure communications,
encryption

Zero-day attack preventions

Inbound TCP/IP port controls

Network segmentation, IDS/IPS

Guards, locks, access controls, monitoring

Applications and Data

Data Security

Patch Management

Intrusion Prevention

Anti-virus

Host-based Firewalls

Server Hardening

Host Security

Internal Network

Network Perimeter

Physical Security

Policies, Procedures, Training

Figure 5.1 Defense in Depth Illustrated

programs, signatures of known bad code (malware) are collected and maintained by AV program developers and redistributed whenever there's an update (which is rather often); this can cause massive disruption of operations and personnel while signature files are updated and rescans of the system are run to detect anything that matches a new signature. We all know that badness is infinite and resists enumeration!

Whitelisting, on the other hand, focuses on "enumerating goodness," which is a far easier and achievable task. Programmers can employ a finite list of what values a variable may contain and reject anything that fails to appear on the list. For example, a common vulnerability in web applications is a failure to check for executable code or HTML tags when input is entered onto a form field. If only alphabetic and numeric characters are expected in a field on the form, the programmer can write code that will cycle through the input character by character to determine if only letters and numbers are present. If there's any input other that numbers and letters, the program should reject the input and force a reentry of the data.

The positive security model can be applied to a number of different application security areas:

- It should be applied to every field of input (hidden or not).
- Validation routines or frameworks should be implemented to specify the characteristics of input that are allowed, as opposed to trying to filter out bad input.
- With access controls, the positive model will deny access to everything, and allow only access to specific authorized resources or functions.

The benefit of using a positive model is that new attacks that have not been anticipated by the developer—including zero-day attacks—can be prevented.

5.5.3 Practice 3: Fail Securely

Handling errors securely is a key aspect of secure and resilient applications. Two major types of errors require special attention:

- Exceptions that occur in the processing of a security control itself
- Exceptions in code that are not "security relevant"

It is important that these exceptions do not enable behavior that a software countermeasure would normally not allow. As a developer, you should consider that there are generally three possible outcomes from a security mechanism:

- Allow the operation.
- Disallow the operation.
- Exception.

In general, you should design your security mechanism so that a failure will follow the same execution path as disallowing the operation. For example, security methods such as "isAuthorized" or "isAuthenticated" should all return false if there is an exception during processing. If security controls can throw exceptions, they must be very clear about exactly what that condition means.

The other type of security-relevant exception is in code that is not part of a security control. These exceptions are security relevant if they affect whether the application properly invokes the control. An exception might cause a security method not to be invoked when it should, or it might affect the initialization of variables used in the security control.

5.5.4 Practice 4: Run with Least Privilege

The principle of least privilege recommends that user accounts have the least amount of privilege required to perform their basic business processes. This encompasses user rights and resource permissions such as

- CPU limits
- Memory
- Network permissions
- File system permissions

The principle of least privilege is widely recognized as an important design consideration in enhancing the protection of data and functionality from faults (i.e., fault tolerance) and malicious behavior (i.e., computer security). The principle of least privilege is also known as the *principle of least authority* (POLA).

5.5.5 Practice 5: Avoid Security by Obscurity

Security by obscurity, as its name implies, describes an attempt to maintain the security of a system or application based on the difficulty in finding or understanding the security mechanisms within it. Security by obscurity relies on the secrecy of the implementation of a system or controls to keep it secure. It is considered a weak security control, and it nearly always fails when it is the only control.

A system that relies on security through obscurity may have theoretical or actual security vulnerabilities, but its owners or designers believe that the flaws are not known and that attackers are unlikely to find them. The technique stands in contrast to security by design.

An example of security by obscurity is a cryptographic system in which the developers wish to keep the algorithm that implements the cryptographic functions a secret, rather than keeping the keys a secret and publishing the algorithm so that security researchers can determine if it is bullet-proof enough for common security uses. This is in direct violation of Kerckhoff's principle from 1883, which states that, "In a well-designed cryptographic system, only the key needs to be secret; there should be no secrecy in the algorithm."[5] Any system that tries to keep its algorithms secret for security reasons is quickly dismissed by the community and is usually referred to as "snake oil" or worse.[6]

5.5.6 Practice 6: Keep Security Simple

Keeping security simple means avoiding overly complex approaches to coding with what would otherwise be relatively straightforward and simple code for someone to read and understand. Developers should avoid the use of double negatives and complex architectures when a simpler approach would be faster. Complexity is the enemy of security!

Keeping security simple is related to a number of other resilience principles and using it as a principle or guideline will help you to meet the spirit of several of the other principles.

One way to keep security simple is to break security functions and features down into these discrete objectives:

1. Keep services running and information away from attackers—related to *deny access by default*.
2. Allow the right users access to the right information—related to *least privilege*.
3. Defend every layer as if it were the last layer of defense—related to *defense in depth*.
4. Keep a record of all attempts to access information (logging).
5. Compartmentalize and isolate resources.

5.5.7 Practice 7: Detect Intrusions

Detecting intrusions in application software requires three elements:

- Capability to log security-relevant events
- Procedures to ensure that logs are monitored regularly
- Procedures to respond properly to an intrusion once it has been detected

Log All Security-Relevant Information

Sometimes you can detect a problem with software by reviewing the log entries that you can't detect at runtime, but you must log enough information to make that possible and useful. In particular, any use of security mechanisms should be logged, with enough information to help track down an offender. In addition, the logging functionality in the application should also provide a method of managing the logged information to prevent tampering or loss.

Ensure That the Logs Are Monitored Regularly

If a security analyst is unable to parse through the event logs to determine which events are actionable, then logging events provide little to no value. Logging provides a forensic function for your application or site.

Respond to Intrusions

Detecting intrusions is important, because otherwise you give the attacker unlimited time to perfect an attack. If you detect intrusions perfectly, then an attacker will get only one attempt before being detected and prevented from launching more attacks.

Should an application receive a request that a legitimate user could not have generated, it is an attack, and your program should respond appropriately.

Never rely on other technologies to detect intrusions. Your code is the only component of the system that has enough information to truly detect attacks. Nothing else will know what parameters are valid, what actions the user is allowed to select, etc. These must be built into the application from the start.

5.5.8 Practice 8: Don't Trust Infrastructure

You'll never know exactly what hardware or operating environment your applications will run on. Relying on a security process or function that may or may not be present is a sure way to have security problems. Make sure that your application's security requirements are explicitly provided through application code or through explicit invocation of reusable security functions provided to application developers to use for the enterprise. We'll cover this more in Chapter 7, Defensive Programming.

5.5.9 Practice 9: Don't Trust Services

Services can refer to any external system. Many organizations use the processing capabilities of third-party partners who likely have different security policies and postures, and it's unlikely that you can influence or control any external third parties, whether they are home users or major suppliers or partners. Therefore, implied trust of externally run systems is not warranted. **All external systems should be treated in a similar fashion.**

For example, a loyalty program provider provides data that is used by Internet banking, providing the number of reward points and a small list of potential redemption items. Within your program that obtains this data, you should check the results to ensure that it is safe to display to end users (does not contain malicious code or actions), and that the reward points are a positive number and not improbably large (data reasonableness).

5.5.10 Practice 10: Establish Secure Defaults

Every application should be delivered *secure by default* out of the box! You should leave it up to users to decide if they can reduce their security if your application allows it. *Secure by default* means that the default configuration settings are the most secure settings possible—not necessarily the most user friendly. For example, password aging and complexity should be enabled by default. Users may be allowed to turn these two features off to simplify their use of the application and increase their risk based on their own risk analysis and policies, but this doesn't force them into an insecure state by default.

5.6 Mapping Best Practices to Nonfunctional Requirements (NFRs) as Acceptance Criteria

Table 5.1 provides a mapping of application security best practices to NFRs needed for secure and resilient applications. Where an X intersects a best practice and an NFR, you'll find a detailed constraint that the application must meet. As you can see, using security controls implements resilience in your

Table 5.1 Nonfunctional Requirements Mapped to Development Best Practices

NFR	Development Best Practice									
	Apply Defense in Depth	Use Positive Security Model	Fail Securely	Run with Least Privilege	Avoid Security by Obscurity	Keep Security Simple	Detect Intrusions	Don't Trust Infrastructure	Don't Trust Services	Establish Secure Defaults
Availability	X	X	X		X	X	X	X	X	X
Capacity	X		X				X			
Efficiency	X	X	X		X	X				X
Extensibility	X	X				X				
Interoperability	X	X		X	X	X				
Manageability	X	X		X	X	X	X			X
Maintainability	X	X	X		X		X			X
Performance	X	X	X	X	X	X	X	X	X	X
Portability	X	X			X	X		X	X	
Privacy	X	X	X	X	X	X	X	X	X	X
Recoverability	X		X		X	X	X			X
Reliability	X	X	X	X	X	X		X	X	X
Scalability	X	X			X	X		X	X	
Security	X	X	X	X	X	X	X	X	X	X
Serviceability	X	X	X		X	X	X			X

application. Because the coverage of practices and NFRs is so dense, applying a security best practice will lead you to solving other non–security-related issues that your Scrum and DevOps teams will most appreciate.

5.7 Summary

In Chapter 5 we explored the critical concepts of security perimeter and attack surface, which led to a list of design and development best practices for secure and resilient application software. With these 10 best practices in mind, you can approach any system design and development problem and understand that security and application resilience—like many other aspects of software engineering—lends itself to a principle-based approach, in which core principles can be applied regardless of implementation technology or application scenario. These principles will serve you well throughout the software development lifecycle.

References

1. Manadhata, P. K., Tan, K. M., Maxion, R. A., and Wing, J. M. (2007, August). An Approach to Measuring a System's Attack Surface. Retrieved from http://www.cs.cmu.edu/~wing/publications/CMU-CS-07-146.pdf
2. Category:Principle. (n.d.). Retrieved from https://www.owasp.org/index.php/Category:Principle
3. Ibid.
4. Sjouwerman, S. (n.d.). Great "Defense-in-Depth" InfoGraphic. Retrieved from https://blog.knowbe4.com/great-defense-in-depth-infographic
5. Encyclopedia: Kerckhoffs' principle. (n.d.). Retrieved from http://www.statemaster.com/encyclopedia/Kerckhoffs%27-principle
6. Crypto-Gram: May 15, 2002. (n.d.). Retrieved from http://www.schneier.com/crypto-gram-0205.html

Chapter 6

Security in the Design Sprint

In Chapter 5, you found 10 best practices and principles for secure and resilient application software development that are used throughout the software development lifecycle (SDLC). In this chapter, you'll see how these principles and best practices are applied in the design efforts of the SDLC, in which the constrained user stories from the earlier work become concrete elements of an overall solution that meets both functional and nonfunctional requirements (NFRs).

6.1 Chapter Overview

Topics you'll find covered in Chapter 6 include details on how to design applications to help meet NFR constraints, how to perform application threat modeling to expose design defects so they are mitigated or countered with different design choices and other security controls, and some rules of thumb that you can use to help you decide where to focus your attention during the design phase. You'll also find a handy checklist at the end of the chapter to encapsulate all the elements of desirable design attributes for application software.

6.2 Design Phase Recommendations

In his white paper "Software Security: Being Insecure in an Insecure World,"[1] Mano Paul offers a number of recommended controls and tools/processes to help meet security and resilience requirements during the various phases of the SDLC. These concepts work very well within the Scrum framework too. Recommendations for the secure design activities cast in Scrum terminology are shown in Table 6.1.

Table 6.1 Design Phase Recommendations

Sprint	Control	How To
Design	• Misuse and abuse • Design/Architecture Reviews • Threat Modeling • NFRs tied to functional user stories	• Evil user stories • Checklists of desirable security design features • Threat Models • Acceptance Criteria and Definition of Done

Even when security and resilience requirements are determined and documented, they often run the risk of being dropped from the backlog or being lost in translation owing to the constraints of time and budget and/or a lack of understanding of their importance by the business or client. Product owners and Scrum masters should plan and allow for time and budget to ensure that these constraints are included in the design work.

6.3 Modeling Misuse Cases

In Chapter 4, you saw how functional requirements of the software are captured as user stories. You can also write evil user stories[2] to express ways you'd like to misuse the application. Here's a few examples:

- **Example #1.** "As a hacker, I can send bad data in URLs, so I can access data and functions for which I'm not authorized."
- **Example #2.** "As a hacker, I can send bad data in the content of requests, so I can access data and functions for which I'm not authorized."
- **Example #3.** "As a hacker, I can send bad data in HTTP headers, so I can access data and functions for which I'm not authorized."
- **Example #4.** "As a hacker, I can read and even modify all data that is input and output by your application."

The authors of the OWASP (Open Web Application Security Project) guidance suggest sneaking these and others like them into the product backlog to spur discussion, but you can achieve the same outcome using *positive security engineering* ideas that build security in, rather than late-stage testing to successively work out defects. That is not to say that software shouldn't be tested—it means that "testing into compliance" is a poor approach for Agile, and a terrible approach if your goal is secure and resilient applications representing your brand and your reputation.

The exercise of mapping how users might interact with an application provides a good understanding of the potential for abuse. A thorough user interaction analysis will identify not only normal use and security attributes, it will also uncover scenarios that the system may not be designed to handle. This is especially useful when users of a system have malicious intent. If potential abuses (or unsupported uses) are not properly considered, vulnerabilities will exist and can be exploited. Use this knowledge you gain to add important information to the acceptance criteria and Definition of Done (DoD).

For security architects and engineers, these scenarios, along with a detailed model for the application's design, are excellent starting points for developing a threat model. In addition, testers can substantially benefit from conducting more robust security tests if they understand all the potential uses of a system.

Another possibly useful tool is a requirements traceability matrix to assist in tracking the misuse cases to the features of the application. This can be performed formally or informally but is helpful in discovering common desirable elements that can be documented as reusable snippets of acceptance criteria across user stories.

6.4 Conduct Security Design and Architecture Reviews in Design Sprint

Everyone recognizes that, in most software development projects, time and budget are fixed values, and the introduction of the "extra work" tied to security and resilience requirements are generally not well received by software development teams (at first), as we discussed in Chapter 2. The best place to introduce the security design and architecture review is when the Scrum team is engaged in the functional design and architecture review of the software.

When conducting a security review, the assurance requirements of the software should be considered, bearing in mind the cost and time constraints and the need for trade-offs. Generating a security plan from the review is a good start for documenting the security design and using it as a check-and-balance guide during and after development. Architecture reviews should be both broad and deep.

Similar to the peer reviews you will find discussed in Chapter 7, architecture and design reviews should include key members of the analysis and design team, the development team, security experts, and SDLC process governance personnel.

6.5 Perform Threat and Application Risk Modeling

Threat modeling includes determining the attack surface of the software by examining its functionality for trust boundaries, entry points, data flow, and exit points. Threat models are only useful once the design documentation that represents the entire application's architecture is more or less finalized, so that the threat model is based on the intended, likely future of the software. Threat modeling is useful for ensuring that the design complements the security objectives, making trade-off and prioritization-of-effort decisions, and reducing the risk of security issues during development and operations. Risk assessments of software can be accomplished by ranking the threats as they pertain to your organization's business objectives, compliance and regulatory requirements, and security exposures. Once understood and prioritized, those newly uncovered threats can then be sent into a phase of planning countermeasures and/or changing the design to remove defects.

An article from MSDN entitled "Lessons Learned from Five Years of Building More Secure Software"[3] underscores the fact that many software security vulnerabilities are actually design defects. When people are exclusively focused on finding security issues in code, that person runs the risk of missing entire classes of vulnerabilities. Security issues in design such as business logic flaws cannot be detected in code and need to be inspected by performing threat models and application risk assessments during the design sprint.

Threat modeling is an iterative-structured technique used to identify the threats to the software under design. Threat modeling breaks the software into physical and logical constructs generating software artifacts that include data flow diagrams, end-to-end deployment scenarios, documented entry and exit points, protocols, components, identities, and services.

Attack surface analysis, as you saw in Chapter 5, is a subset of threat modeling and can be performed when generating the software context to zero-in on the parts of the software that are exposed to untrusted users. These areas are then analyzed for security issues. Once the software context is generated, pertinent threats and vulnerabilities can be identified.

Threat modeling is performed during design work so that necessary security controls and countermeasures can be defined for the development phase of the software. OWASP[4] describes the benefits of threat modeling:

- Builds a secure design
- Efficient investment of resources; appropriately prioritize security, development, and other tasks
- Brings security and development together to collaborate on a shared understanding, informing development of the system
- Identifies threats and compliance requirements and evaluates their risk

- Defines the need for required controls
- Balances risks, controls, and usability
- Identifies where building a control is unnecessary, based on acceptable risk
- Documents threats and mitigation
- Ensures that business requirements (or goals) are adequately protected in the face of a malicious actor, accidents, or other causes of impact
- Identifies specific types of security tests and scenarios to test the application under the acceptance criteria dictates

SANS Institute Cyber Defense offers a handy seven-step recipe[5] for conducting threat modeling and application risk analysis. The recipe is as follows:

Step 1: Make a list of what you're trying to protect.
Step 2: Draw a diagram and add notes.
Step 3: Make a list of your adversaries and what they want.
Step 4: Brainstorm threats from these adversaries.
Step 5: Estimate probability and potential damage (the overall risk).
Step 6: Brainstorm countermeasures and their issues.
Step 7: Plan, test, pilot, monitor, troubleshoot and repeat.

Detailed directions for each of these steps is provided at the site, along with a spreadsheet template you can use for data collection and analysis. We'll look at some of the details behind how Steps 4, 5, and 6 are performed.

6.5.1 Brainstorming Threats

Step 4 of the recipe calls for brainstorming threats from your adversaries. One of the more popular brainstorming techniques was popularized by Microsoft and is called STRIDE.
STRIDE stands for:

- Spoofing
- Tampering
- Repudiation
- Information disclosure
- Denial of service
- Elevation of privilege

The central idea behind STRIDE is that you can classify all your threats according to one of the six STRIDE categories. Because each category has a specific set of potential mitigations, once you have analyzed the threats, categorized them, and prioritized them, you will know how to mitigate or eliminate the defect that could lead to an exploit.

- **Spoofing.** A spoofing attack occurs when an attacker pretends to be someone they are not. An attacker using DNS hijacking and pretending to be www.microsoft.com would be an example of a spoofing attack.
- **Tampering.** Tampering attacks occur when the attacker modifies data in transit. An attacker that modified a TCP stream by predicting the sequence numbers would be tampering with those data flows. Obviously, data stores can be tampered with—that is what happens when the attacker writes specially crafted data into a file to exploit a vulnerability.
- **Repudiation.** Repudiation occurs when someone performs an action and then claims that they did not actually perform it. Primarily this shows up on activities such as credit card transactions: a user purchases something and then claims that they did not. Another way that this shows up is in email—if I receive an email from you, you can claim that you never sent it.
- **Information disclosure.** Information disclosure threats are usually quite straightforward: can the attacker view data that they are not entitled to view? When you are transferring data from one computer to another over a network, if the attacker can pull the data off the wire, then your component is subject to an information disclosure threat. Data stores are also subject to information disclosure threats: if an unauthorized person can read the contents of the file, it is an information disclosure issue.
- **Denial of service.** Denial of service threats occur when an attacker can degrade or deny service to users. If an attacker can crash your component, redirect packets into a black hole, or consume all the CPU on the box, you have a denial of service situation.
- **Elevation of privilege.** An elevation of privilege threat occurs when an attacker has the ability to gain privileges that they would not normally have. One of the reasons that classic buffer overflows are so important is that they often allow an attacker to raise their privilege level—for instance, a buffer overflow in any Internet facing component allows an attacker to elevate their privilege level from anonymous to the local user.

The STRIDE process is really a brainstorming activity conducted in person or via media sharing channels (e.g., WebEx). Participants use the documentation to identify assets in the architecture, their purpose, and their relative value. These become the targets for would-be attackers.

Next, identify possible attackers and what they would want from the system:

- Who are your actual or likely adversaries?
- What do they want to achieve?

- What are their skills and resources?
- How determined are they?
- What would they be willing to risk or give up in order to achieve their goals?
- What about insiders?

As you collect these across projects, you can also build a reusable catalog of attack profiles with enough detail to make them suitable for anyone who wants to conduct threat modeling.

Next, imagine that you are one of those adversaries and try to see your network *through their eyes.* You know what you want; how would you try to get at it by misusing the application?

Just like the product backlog and user stories, a threat model is a living document—as you change the design, you need to go back and update your threat model to see if any new threats appear.

6.6 Risk Analysis and Assessment

For Step 5 of the recipe, we turn to another mnemonic from Microsoft, called DREAD. It scores 5 categories,[6] which are added together and divided by 5, yielding a result from 0–10, where 0 indicates little or no impact and 10 is the house-on-fire situation:

```
Risk Outcome = (DAMAGE POTENTIAL + REPRODUCIBILITY +
EXPLOITABILITY + AFFECTED USERS + DISCOVERABILITY) / 5
```

6.6.1 Damage Potential

If the vulnerability is exploited, how much damage will be caused?

0 = Nothing

3 = Individual user data is compromised or affected or availability denied

5 = A subset of data is compromised or affected or availability denied

7 = All data is compromised or affected, or its availability denied

7 = Availability of a specific component/service is denied

8 = Availability of all components is denied

9 = Underlying infrastructure data is compromised or affected

10 = Complete system or data destruction, failure, or compromise

6.6.2 Reproducibility

How reliably can the vulnerability be exploited?

0 = Very hard or impossible, even for administrators. The vulnerability is unstable or statistically unlikely to be reliably exploited.

5 = Some extra steps are required; tooling/scripting readily available.

10 = Unauthenticated users can trivially and reliably exploit using only a Web browser.

6.6.3 Exploitability

How difficult is the vulnerability to exploit?

0 = N/A (The assertion here is that every vulnerability is exploitable, given time and effort. All scores should be 1–10.)

1 = Even with direct knowledge of the vulnerability, we do not see a viable path for exploitation.

2 = Advanced techniques are required, bespoke tooling. Only exploitable by authenticated users.

5 = Exploit is available/understood, usable with only moderate skill by authenticated users.

7 = Exploit is available/understood, usable by non-authenticated users.

10 = Trivial—just a web browser.

6.6.4 Affected Users

How many users will be affected?

0 = None

5 = Specific to a given project

10 = All users impacted

6.6.5 Discoverability

How easy is it to discover the threat, to learn of the vulnerability?

0 = Very hard to impossible to detect even given access to source code and privilege access to running systems.

5 = Can figure it out by guessing or by monitoring network traces.

9 = Details of faults like this are already in the public domain and can be easily discovered using a search engine.

10 = The information is visible in the web browser address bar or in a form.

Table 6.2[7] gives an example of what this might look like for a tampering and privilege escalation threat scenario.

Table 6.2 Example DREAD Scoring Sheet

Threat Identified: Threat ID nnn — Tampering, Privilege Escalation		
Category	Score	Rationale
Damage	6	Significant disruption
Reproducibility	8	Code path is easily understood, condition exists in legacy code
Exploitability	2	Difficult as application is implemented
Affected Users	8	All cloud computing users
Discoverability	10	Assumed to be 10
DREAD SCORE: 31/5 = 6.2 – Important — fix as priority		

You use this approach for each of the threats you identified in Step 4, then sort the outcomes in descending order of DREAD score to address those risks with the highest risks first.

6.7 Don't Forget These Risks!

Other risk analysis considerations include:

- Threats and vulnerabilities that exist in the project's environment or that result from interaction with other systems.
- Code that was created by external development groups in either source or object form. It's vitally important to evaluate carefully any code from sources external to your team, including purchased libraries and Open Source components and libraries that may be present. Failing to do so might cause security vulnerabilities the team does not know about or learns about too late.
- Threat models should include all legacy code if the project is a new release of an existing program. Such code could have been written before much was known about software security, and therefore it likely contains vulnerabilities.

- A detailed privacy analysis to document your project's key privacy aspects. Important issues to consider include:
  - What personal data is collected?
  - What is the compelling customer value proposition and business justification?
  - What notice and consent experiences are provided?
  - What controls are provided to both internal and external users of the application?
  - How is unauthorized access to personal information prevented?

6.8 Rules of Thumb for Defect Removal or Mitigation

To help you guide your thinking about what kinds of threats deserve remediation or mitigation, here are some rules of thumb to use while performing your threat modeling.

- If the data has not crossed a trust boundary, you do not really need to care about it.
- If the threat requires that the attacker is already running code on the client at your privilege level, you do not really need to care about it.
- If your code runs with any elevated privileges, you **need** to be concerned.
- If your code invalidates assumptions made by other entities, you **need** to be concerned.
- If your code listens on the network, you **need** to be concerned.
- If your code retrieves information from the Internet, you **need** to be concerned.
- If your code deals with data that came from a file, you **need** to be concerned.
- If your code is marked as safe for scripting or safe for initialization, you **need** to be concerned.

6.9 Further Needs for Information Assurance

In today's world it's vital to engineer an application with enough security and resilience controls and constraints that provide the following:

- Assurance that users and client applications are identified and that their identities are properly verified
- Assurance that users and client applications can only access data and services for which they have been properly authorized

- Ability to detect attempted intrusions by unauthorized people and client applications
- Assurance that unauthorized malicious programs (e.g., viruses) do not infect the application or component
- Assurance that communications and data are not intentionally corrupted
- Assurance that parties to interactions with the application or component cannot later repudiate those interactions
- Assurance that confidential communications and data are kept private
- Ability for security personnel to audit the status and usage of the security mechanisms
- Assurance that applications can survive attack or operate in a degraded mode
- Assurance that system maintenance does not unintentionally disrupt the security mechanisms of the application or any of its components

Once your threat identification and prioritization steps are completed, you should have the following sets of information available for the next steps of identifying different design choices, countermeasures that should be added, and improvements in the design based on the reviews. Completed threat-model documentation should include:

- A diagram and an enumeration and description of the elements in your diagram.
- A threat and risk analysis, because that is the core of the threat model.
- For each mitigated threat that you identify in the threat analysis, you should include the bug or defect number associated with the mitigation plan to add to your backlog of required work.
- You should also have a one- or two-paragraph description of your software components and what they do. Maintaining a list of key contacts for questions is also useful.
- Confirm that threat model data and associated documentation (functional/design specifications) is stored using the document control system used by the development team.
- You should consider reviews and approvals of threat models and referenced mitigations reviewed by at least one developer, one tester, and one program or project manager. Ask architects, developers, testers, program managers, and others who understand the software to contribute to the threat models and to review them. Solicit broad input and reviews to ensure the threat models are as comprehensive as possible.

And remember that threat modeling is never complete as long as the application continues to gain features, is ported to other operating environments (e.g., the cloud) or is re-written as web services and microservices to take advantage of modern computing practices.

6.10 Countering Threats through Proactive Controls

In 2018, OWASP released the OWASP Top 10 Proactive Controls[8] as a set of security techniques that should be included in every software development project. They are ordered by importance, with control number 1 being the most important, and they appear in Figure 6.1.

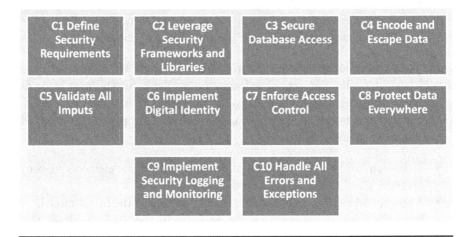

Figure 6.1   OWASP Top 10 Proactive Controls (*Source:* OWASP, licensed under Creative Commons BY-SA)

The document is delivered as a PDF that's useful for the Scrum team in helping to formulate alternative design choices to reduce risks or add compensating controls that mitigate the threat, should it actually be exploited. The document serves as guidance and advice that can speed up the process of researching controls to counter threats. Figure 6.2 shows the structure and content for each of the controls in the catalog.

6.11 Architecture and Design Review Checklist

The OWASP Secure Application Design Project offers an architecture and design review checklist that covers most security and resilience aspects of the architecture and design stages of the SDLC, including the following areas:

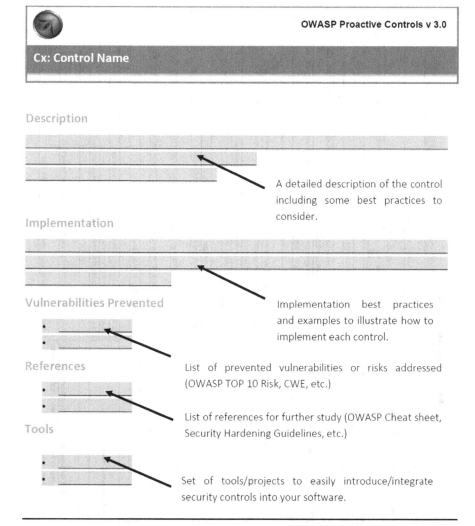

Figure 6.2 Structure of OWASP Top 10 Proactive Controls Documentation (*Source:* OWASP, licensed under Creative Commons BY-SA)

- Authentication
- Authorization
- Configuration management
- Sensitive data
- Session management
- Cryptography
- Parameter manipulation
- Exception management
- Auditing and logging

Checklist for Securing Application Design

Category	Vulnerable Area	Facts to ANALYSE
Design		
Code Flow – Division of code based on MVC	Presence of backdoor parameters/functions/files	1. Are there backdoor/unexposed business logic classes?
		2. Are there unused configurations related to business logic?
		3. If request parameters are used to identify business logic methods, is there a proper mapping of user privileges and methods/actions allowed to them?
	Placement of checks	1. Are security checks placed before processing inputs?
	Insecure Data Binding Mechanism	1. Check if unexposed instance variables are present in form objects that get bound to user inputs. If present, check if they have default values.
		2. Check if unexposed instance variables present in form objects that get bound to user inputs. If present, check if they get initialized before form binding.
	Insecure authentication and access control logic	1. Is the placement of authentication and authorization check correct?
		2. Is there execution stopped/terminated after for invalid request? I.e. when authentication/authorization check fails?
		3. Are the checks correct implemented? Is there any backdoor parameter?
		4. Is the check applied on all the required files and folder within web root directory?
Authentication and Access Control Mechanism	Redundant configuration	1. Is there any default configuration like Access- ALL?
		2. Does the configuration get applied to all files and users?
		3. Incase of container managed authentication - Is the authentication based on web methods only?
		4. Incase of container managed authentication - Does the authentication get applied on all resources?
	Insecure Session management	1. Does the design handle sessions securely?
	Weak Password Handling	1. Is Password Complexity Check enforced on the password?
		2. Is password stored in an encrypted format?
		3. Is password disclosed to user/written to a file/logs/console?
Data Access Mechanism	Presence of sensitive data in configuration/code files	1. Are database credentials stored in an encrypted format?
	Presence/support for different insecure data sources and their related flaws	1. Does the design support weak datastores like flat files

	Centralized Validation and Interceptors	**Weakness in any existing security control**	1. Does the centralized validation get applied to all requests and all the inputs? 2. Does the centralized validation check block all the special characters? 3. Does are there any special kind of request skipped from validation? 4. Does the design maintain any exclusion list for parameters or features from being validated?
Architecture	**Entry Points**	**Insecure Data handling and validation**	1. Are all the untrusted inputs validated?
	External Integrations	**Insecure data transmission**	1. Is the data sent on encrypted channel? Does the application use HTTPClient for making external connections? 2. Does the design involve session sharing between components/modules? Is session validated correctly on both ends?
		Elevated privilege levels	1. Does the design use any elevated OS/system privileges for external connections/commands?
	External API's used	**Known flaws present in 3rd party APIs/functions**	1. Is there any known flaw in API's/Technology used? For eg: DWR
Configuration	**Inbuilt Security Controls**	**Common Security Controls**	1. Does the design framework provide any inbuilt security control? Like <%: %> in ASP.NET MVC. 2. Are are there any flaw/weakness in the existing inbuilt control? 3. Are all security setting enabled in the design?

Ashish Rao
Ph: 91-9819080470
rao.ashish20@gmail.com
Blog: http://artechtalks.blogspot.in/

Figure 6.3   OWASP Secure Application Design Proejct Checklist (*Source:* OWASP, licensed under Creative Commons BY-SA)

(*Note:* A description of Figure 6.3 can be found on page 88.)

Use this checklist (Figure 6.3) to help you conduct architecture and design reviews to evaluate the security of your web applications and to implement the design guidelines we described in Chapter 5.

This checklist should evolve based on the experience you gain from performing reviews and may need to be extended now and then to accommodate new approaches to application development and operations, including microservices, web services, IoT, and cloud migrations.

6.12 Summary

Chapter 6 offers a number of recommendations and tools to use for software design to help meet NFRs related to security and resilience. You were also offered some reasons and tips on how to conduct threat modeling and application risk analysis, along with its process steps and tools for exercises. Finally, you were provided a useful checklist to use when conducting architecture and design analysis activities.

In Chapter 7, we will use the outcomes from these now-secured design models and patterns and choices as the basis for developing secure and resilient consistently.

References

1. Paul, M. (2009, January). (ISC) 2: Software Security: Being Secure in an Insecure World. White paper, *Global Security Magazine.* Available at https://www.global securitymag.fr/Mano-Paul-ISC-2-Software-Security,20090122,7114.html
2. Agile Software Development: Don't Forget EVIL User Stories. (n.d.). Retrieved from https://www.owasp.org/index.php/Agile_Software_Development:_Don% 27t_Forget_EVIL_User_Stories
3. Threat Modeling Again, Pulling the Threat Model Together. (2007, September 14). Retrieved from http://blogs.msdn.com/larryosterman/archive/2007/09/14/threat-modeling-again-pulling-the-threat-model-together.aspx
4. Application Threat Modeling. (n.d.). Retrieved from https://www.owasp.org/index.php/Application_Threat_Modeling
5. Cyber Defense. (2009, July 11). Retrieved from https://cyber-defense.sans.org/blog/2009/07/11/practical-risk-analysis-spreadsheet/
6. Security/OSSA-Metrics. (n.d.). Retrieved from https://wiki.openstack.org/wiki/Security/OSSA-Metrics#DREAD
7. Ibid.
8. OWASP Proactive Controls. (n.d.). Retrieved from https://www.owasp.org/index.php/OWASP_Proactive_Controls

Chapter 7

Defensive Programming

You've seen how to select and apply concepts and principles of security and resilience from the very start of product development. You saw how to map the best practices to nonfunctional requirements (NFR)s to prove that minding the security of an application brings along for the ride most of the other characteristics you find desirable in high-quality software. In Chapters 5 and 6, you saw how to apply these practices in the design work of the software development lifecycle (SDLC) to set the stage for programming best practices and techniques found in this chapter.

7.1 Chapter Overview

Defensive programming is exactly what it sounds like. Before you're handed the keys to your first car (one would hope), someone insisted that you take a driver's education and responsibilities class, usually in a simulator, and when on the road, always with an instructor who had a steering wheel and brake to keep people from getting killed while you're learning how to drive in the real world. When you're ticketed for relatively minor offenses, you're usually offered the chance to make the ticket go away if you successfully complete a defensive driving course to remind you of traffic laws and reinforce your duty and responsibility to drive defensively at all times.

Programming is not that much different. Programs today are under regular attack if they happen to have any Internet access. Programs cannot defend themselves unless they're taught how to from the very first line of code typed. Role-based education in defensive programming techniques, as you saw in Chapter 3, is the avenue to reliably gaining those skills, and its importance cannot be overemphasized!

Programmers today have an awesome responsibility to *get it right the first time,* because their work could adversely affect life and limb. Not that long ago, before software was used to control millions of kinetic machines and devices on our streets, in our homes, and in our bodies, when an application crashed or its control was lost, a restart usually fixed the issue. Today when software crashes, it could indeed lead to a real crash that kills real people.

Ethics also play an important role in today's software development world. In the case of autonomous vehicles, how should a program work in the face of an imminent threat that's unavoidable, protect the passenger in the vehicle, or minimize the damage outside the vehicle? Choices made in software dictate this type of behavior. Will consumers and users of self-driving cars ever know what those choices are before it's too late?

With that sense of awesome responsibility in mind, Chapter 7 offers guidance and paradigms for secure programming practices that improve software quality while enhancing its resilience features. This chapter is primarily intended for development (coding) staff, but it is useful for appsec architects to use as guidance to Scrum teams who need specific details on recognizing and remediating security-related programming defects and to supplement their formal training.

7.2 The Evolution of Attacks

Attack techniques evolve over time. Secure design and programming best practices have always been the best form of defense against these attacks—some of them have proven themselves capable of later defending attacks that had not yet been identified.

Dan Kaminsky[1] discovered in the summer of 2008 a serious vulnerability in the domain name servers (DNS) that could allow attackers to redirect clients to alternate servers of their own choosing, leading to potential misuse. Years earlier, a cryptographer named Daniel J. Bernstein[2] looked at DNS security and decided that source port randomization was a smart design choice by the designers of DNS. The work-around that was rolled out following Kaminsky's discovery used the source port randomization feature to counter the problem. Bernstein did not know about Kaminsky's attack, but he understood and envisioned a general class of attacks and realized that this enhancement could protect against them. Consequently, the DNS program he wrote in 2000, djbdns,[3] did not need any patching—it was already immune to Kaminsky's attack.

This is what a good design looks like—it is not just secure against known attacks; it is also secure against unknown or zero-day attacks.

Even with good designs, there are multiple ways a developer who implements the design can introduce vulnerabilities into the process, thus making the entire system insecure. This chapter explains some of the common vulnerabilities (with a focus on custom web applications that are the key targets of today's attacks) and provides some best practices and secure coding concepts to protect against them.

7.3 Threat and Vulnerability Taxonomies

Different people look at software defects in different ways. Some see security programming defects as vulnerabilities and others see defects as weaknesses. Still others see them as programming errors.

We're going to take a look at the two of the dominant taxonomies that application security tool developers use to indicate defects or refer to using common names for well-known vulnerabilities.

7.3.1 MITRE's Common Weaknesses Enumeration (CWE™)

Intended for both the development community and the community of security practitioners, Common Weakness Enumeration (CWE)[4] is a formal list or dictionary of common software weaknesses that can occur in software's architecture, design, code, or implementation and can lead to exploitable security vulnerabilities.

CWE was created to serve as a common language to describe software security weaknesses; serve as a standard measuring stick for software security tools targeting these weaknesses; and provide a common baseline standard for weakness identification, mitigation, and prevention efforts.

Software weaknesses are flaws, faults, bugs, vulnerabilities, and other errors in software implementation, code, design, or architecture that, if left unaddressed, could result in systems and networks being vulnerable to attack.

Some example software weaknesses include:

- Buffer overflows
- Format strings
- Structure and validity problems
- Common special element manipulations
- Channel and path errors
- Handler errors

- User interface errors
- Pathname traversal and equivalence errors
- Authentication errors
- Resource management errors
- Insufficient verification of data
- Code evaluation and injection
- Randomness and predictability

What's important to know about CWE at this point is that it's the "language" that you'll most likely encounter as you work with software security scanners and other tools. CWE is not only an awareness tool, it's also a set of recommended practices to prevent or remediate the defect it refers to. Think of CWE as a superset of known weaknesses in programming and design, collected as a dictionary. We'll talk much more about CWEs in Chapters 8 and 9 on testing.

7.3.2 OWASP Top 10—2017

The Open Web Application Security Project (OWASP) is an open community dedicated to enabling organizations to develop, purchase, and maintain applications that can be trusted. "Community" includes corporations, educational organizations, and individuals from around the world with the focus on creating freely available articles, open methodologies, documentation, tools, and technologies to improve web software security.

The OWASP Top 10[5] is a list of the 10 most severe web security issues as defined and regularly updated by the OWASP community:

- Addresses issues with applications on the perimeter of an organization and accessed by external parties
- Widely accepted and referenced as mandatory by:
  - U.S. Federal Trade Commission
  - U.S. Defense Information Systems Agency (U.S. Department of Defense)
  - Payment Card Industry Data Security Standard (PCI-DSS)

The OWASP Top 10 is a powerful awareness document for web application security.

The current version (at the time of writing this chapter) is the 2017 OWASP Top 10. The OWASP Top 10 has always been about risk, but the 2017 update is clearer than previous editions and provides additional information on how to assess these risks in your applications.

The 2017 OWASP Top 10 Most Critical Web Application Security Risks are:

- **A1: 2017-Injection.** Injection flaws, such as SQL, NoSQL, OS, and LDAP injection, occur when untrusted data is sent to an interpreter as part of a command or query. The attacker's hostile data can trick the interpreter into executing unintended commands or accessing data without proper authorization.
- **A2: 2017-Broken Authentication.** Application functions related to authentication and session management are often implemented incorrectly, allowing attackers to compromise passwords, keys, or session tokens or to exploit other implementation flaws to assume other users' identities temporarily or permanently.
- **A3: 2017-Sensitive Data Exposure.** Many web applications and APIs do not properly protect sensitive data, such as financial, healthcare, and PII. Attackers may steal or modify such weakly protected data to conduct credit card fraud, identity theft, or other crimes. Sensitive data may be compromised without extra protection, such as encryption at rest or in transit, and requires special precautions when exchanged with the browser.
- **A4: 2017-XML External Entities (XXE).** Many older or poorly configured XML processors evaluate external entity references within XML documents. External entities can be used to disclose internal files using the file URI handler, internal file shares, internal port scanning, remote code execution, and denial of service attacks.
- **A5: 2017-Broken Access Control.** Restrictions on what authenticated users are allowed to do are often not properly enforced. Attackers can exploit these flaws to access unauthorized functionality and/or data, such as access other users' accounts, view sensitive files, modify other users' data, change access rights, etc.
- **A6: 2017-Security Misconfiguration.** Security misconfiguration is the most commonly seen issue. This is typically a result of insecure default configurations, incomplete or ad hoc configurations, open cloud storage, misconfigured HTTP headers, and verbose error messages containing sensitive information. Not only must all operating systems, frameworks, libraries, and applications be securely configured, but they must be patched and upgraded in a timely fashion.
- **A7: 2017-Cross-Site Scripting (XSS).** XSS flaws occur whenever an application either includes untrusted data in a new web page without proper validation or escaping, or updates an existing web page with user-supplied data using a browser API that can create HTML or JavaScript. XSS allows attackers to execute scripts in the victim's browser, which can hijack user sessions, deface websites, or redirect the user to malicious sites.
- **A8: 2017-Insecure Deserialization.** Insecure deserialization often leads to remote code execution. Even if deserialization flaws do not result in

remote code execution, they can be used to perform attacks, including replay attacks, injection attacks, and privilege escalation attacks.

- **A9: 2017-Using Components with Known Vulnerabilities.** Components, such as libraries, frameworks, and other software modules, run with the same privileges as the application. If a vulnerable component is exploited, such an attack can facilitate serious data loss or server takeover. Applications and APIs using components with known vulnerabilities may undermine application defenses and enable various attacks and impacts

- **A10: 2017-Insufficient Logging & Monitoring.** Insufficient logging and monitoring, coupled with missing or ineffective integration with incident response, allows attackers to further attack systems, maintain persistence, pivot to more systems, and tamper, extract, or destroy data. Most breach studies show that time to detect a breach is over 200 days, typically detected by external parties rather than internal processes or monitoring.

Notice that the Top 10 is just a small subset of CWEs mentioned earlier. The OWASP Top 10 addresses the most impactful application security risks currently facing organizations. It's based primarily on over 40 data submissions from firms that specialize in application security, and an industry survey that was completed by over 500 individuals. This data spans vulnerabilities gathered from hundreds of organizations and over 100,000 real-world applications and APIs. The Top 10 items are selected and prioritized according to this prevalence data, in combination with consensus estimates of exploitability, detectability, and impact.

Although static code scanners provide filters to filter out defects (CWEs) that are not represented in the Top 10, these scanners are NOT looking specifically for these vulnerabilities. What the scanners do is attribute the vulnerabilities it finds back to the common taxonomies, such as the CWE and OWASP Top 10, but they will find most known vulnerabilities present in the code. Scanner output is made manageable and usable by filtering and sorting to find those vulnerabilities you care about the most and need to address.

With a language and taxonomy to talk about defects and vulnerabilities, conversations lead to common understanding that, in turn, leads to positive discussions on addressing and treating defects. Programmers are well advised to gain a good understanding of CWE and OWASP Top 10 as they begin to address appsec concerns.

7.4 Failure to Sanitize Inputs is the Scourge of Software Development

One common theme of the OWASP Top 10 is injection-related attacks, where user-entered commands modify how a program operates when the application uses these inputs to run their own code. In essence, if an attacker can usurp control of the program using their own input, the program is no longer yours. Preventing injection attacks—every time, on every input—using the advice and guidance you'll find below will eliminate most of the injection-based vulnerabilities.

7.5 Input Validation and Handling

Improper input handling[6] is one of the most common weaknesses identified across applications today. Poorly handled input is a leading cause of critical vulnerabilities that exist in systems and applications.

When attacking an application, a malicious user will attempt to supply unexpected data through its input parameters in order to cause an error condition or get their code to run. For this reason, **every input data element** received by the application should be validated before being used. A typical example of input that should be validated is the data the user supplies on a form's text fields. However, you should validate **any** input coming from the user's browser, because the attacker could supply malicious instructions from anywhere as input to gain unauthorized access to the application or its data. Your application will not know if the messages are coming from a browser or are being edited by a browser proxy. For this reason, any validation that's done on the client (browser) is easily circumvented, so it's essential that ALL official validation be performed on the server.

Typical developers underestimate what really constitutes input to an application. There is usually much more than what the developer expects. For a web application, input could be any of the following:

- All HTML form fields
- Included form fields that do not seem to be modifiable by the user:
  - Checkboxes
  - Radio buttons
  - Select lists
  - Hidden fields
- All links that contain hard-coded query string parameters
- All cookies used by an application
- HTTP response headers

In general, you should consider **any** data coming from outside the application security perimeter (trust boundary) as a potential threat. This includes anything coming directly from the user's browser and anything coming from other applications or external databases or files, because the security of these elements is beyond the application's control. Even if data coming from external sources could be trusted to a certain degree, the "fail safe" approach is to validate all input data.

Why Input Validation Is Fundamental

Anything that is displayed on a browser, and most of what is not displayed, is threatened by unauthorized modifications or deliberate manipulation from malevolent users. The family of software called "browser proxies" can turn an innocuous web browser into a powerful tool that can circumvent all client-side (browser-based) input validation activity. One popular tool in this family is called Burp Suite,[7] available at Portswigger.net. Burp is configured through the browser to stop and trap all traffic flowing from the browser to the ISP and back. Each request and response message can be viewed on an intercept screen and then edited on a subsequent screen that presents a tabular view of the traffic flow. Figure 7.1 contains a summary of the things you can do with Burp Suite.

So, what can you do with a browser proxy? When you submit a form to the web server after filling it out, Burp will give you the option to review the message and payload and let you change it to your heart's content before you forward the message to the application for processing. Changes could be made to the price of an item in the case of e-commerce and where the programmers did not know any better than to implement the function securely, or changes could be made to inject commands or malicious input to force the application to crash or behave in ways the programmer never intended.

In general, the term *input handing* is used to describe functions such as validation, cleansing, sanitizing, filtering, encoding and/or decoding of input data. Applications receive input from various sources, including human users, software agents (browsers), files, and network/peripheral devices, to name a few. In the case of web applications, input can be transferred in various formats (name value pairs, JavaScript Object Notation [JSON], Simple Object Access Protocol [SOAP], web services, etc.) and obtained via URL query strings, POST data, HTTP headers, cookies, etc. We can obtain non-web application input via application variables, environment variables, the registry, configuration files, etc. Regardless of the data format or source/location of the input, all input from outside the application's security perimeter or trust boundary should be considered explicitly untrusted and potentially malicious. Applications that process untrusted input may become vulnerable to attacks such as buffer overflows, SQL injection, OS commanding, and denial of service, just to name a few.

One of the key aspects of input handling is validating that the input satisfies a certain criterion. For proper validation, it is important to identify the form

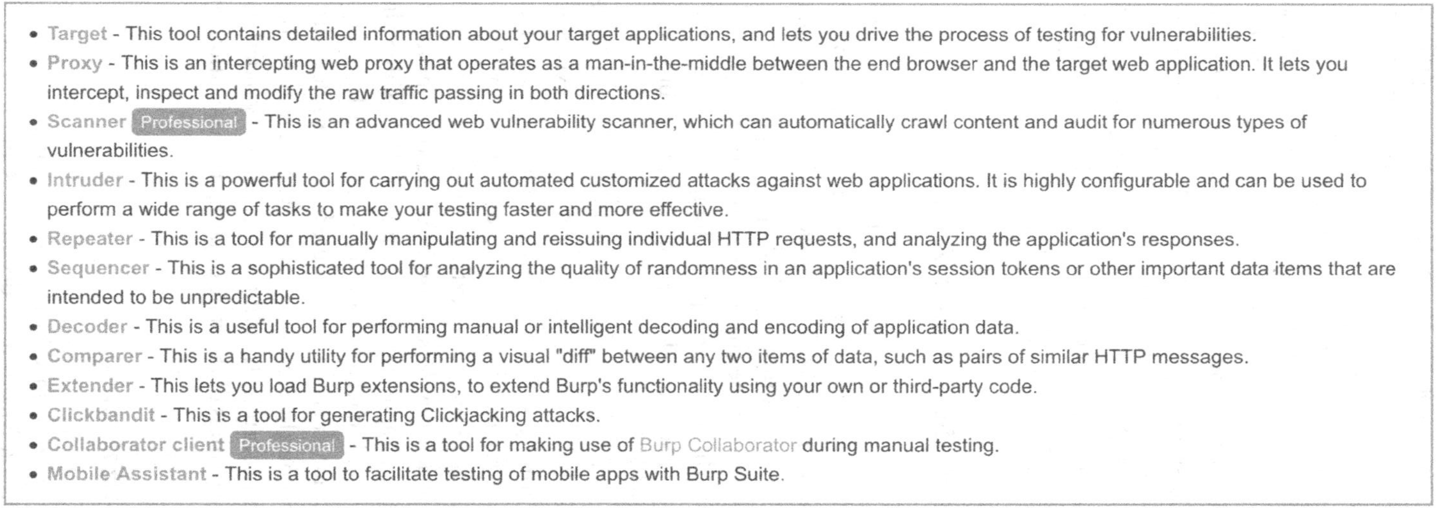

- Target - This tool contains detailed information about your target applications, and lets you drive the process of testing for vulnerabilities.
- Proxy - This is an intercepting web proxy that operates as a man-in-the-middle between the end browser and the target web application. It lets you intercept, inspect and modify the raw traffic passing in both directions.
- Scanner `Professional` - This is an advanced web vulnerability scanner, which can automatically crawl content and audit for numerous types of vulnerabilities.
- Intruder - This is a powerful tool for carrying out automated customized attacks against web applications. It is highly configurable and can be used to perform a wide range of tasks to make your testing faster and more effective.
- Repeater - This is a tool for manually manipulating and reissuing individual HTTP requests, and analyzing the application's responses.
- Sequencer - This is a sophisticated tool for analyzing the quality of randomness in an application's session tokens or other important data items that are intended to be unpredictable.
- Decoder - This is a useful tool for performing manual or intelligent decoding and encoding of application data.
- Comparer - This is a handy utility for performing a visual "diff" between any two items of data, such as pairs of similar HTTP messages.
- Extender - This lets you load Burp extensions, to extend Burp's functionality using your own or third-party code.
- Clickbandit - This is a tool for generating Clickjacking attacks.
- Collaborator client `Professional` - This is a tool for making use of Burp Collaborator during manual testing.
- Mobile Assistant - This is a tool to facilitate testing of mobile apps with Burp Suite.

Figure 7.1 Burp Suite Features (*Source:* PortSwigger Web Security. Reproduced with permission.)

and type of data that is acceptable and expected by the application. Defining an expected format and usage of each instance of untrusted input is required to accurately define restrictions.

Validation can include checks for variable-type safety (e.g., integer, floating point, text) and syntax correctness. String input should be checked for length (minimum and maximum number of characters) and "character set" validation, by which numeric input types such as integers and decimals can be validated against acceptable upper and lower bounds of values. When combining input from multiple sources, validation should be performed on the concatenated result and not only against the individual data elements alone. This practice helps avoid situations in which input validation may succeed when performed on individual data items but fail when done on a concatenated string from all the sources.[8]

7.5.1 Client-Side vs. Server-Side Validation

A common mistake, mentioned earlier, that developers make is to include validation routines in the client-side of an application using JavaScript functions as a *sole* means of performing bounds checking. Validation routines that are beneficial on the client side cannot be relied upon to provide a security control, because all data accessible on the client side is modifiable by a malicious user or attacker, as you saw with the browser proxy tool. This is true of any client-side validation checks in JavaScript and VBScript or external browser plug-ins such as Flash, Java, or ActiveX.

The HTML Version 5 specification has added a new attribute "pattern" to the INPUT tag that enables developers to write regular expressions as part of the markup for performing validation checks.[9] Although this feature makes it even more convenient for developers to perform input validation on the client side without having to write any extra code, the risk from such a feature becomes significant when developers use it as the only means of performing input validation for their applications. **Relying on client-side validation *alone* is bad practice**. Although client-side validation is great for user interface (UI) and functional validation, it is not a substitute for server-side security validation. Performing validation on the server side is the ONLY way to assure the integrity of your validation controls. In addition, server-side validation routines will always be effective, regardless of the state of JavaScript execution on the browser.

7.5.2 Input Sanitization

Sanitizing input can be performed by transforming input from its original form to an acceptable form via encoding or decoding. Common encoding methods used in web applications include HTML entity encoding and URL encoding schemes. HTML entity encoding serves the need for encoding literal representations of certain meta-characters to their corresponding character entity references. Character references for HTML entities are pre-defined and have the format "&name", where "name" is a case-sensitive alphanumeric string. A common example of HTML entity encoding is where "<" is encoded as < and ">" is encoded as >. URL encoding applies to parameters and their associated values that are transmitted as part of HTTP query strings. Likewise, characters that are not permitted in URLs are represented using their Unicode character set code point value, where each byte is encoded in hexadecimal as "%HH". For example, "<" is URL-encoded as "%3C" and ">" is URL-encoded as "%CE".

There are multiple ways that input can be presented to an application. With web applications and browsers supporting multiple character encoding types, it has become commonplace for attackers to try to exploit inherent weaknesses in encoding and decoding routines. Applications requiring internationalization are a good candidate for input sanitization. One of the common forms of representing international characters is Unicode. Unicode transformations use the Universal Character Set (UCS), which consists of a large set of characters to cover symbols of almost all the languages in the world. From the most novice developer to the most seasoned security expert and developer, rarely do programmers write routines that inspect every character within a Unicode string to confirm its validity. Such misrepresentation of characters enables attackers to spoof expected values by replacing them with visually or semantically similar characters from the UCS.

7.5.3 Canonicalization

Canonicalization is another important aspect of input sanitization. Canonicalization deals with converting data with various possible representations into a standard "canonical" representation deemed acceptable by the application. One of the most commonly known applications of canonicalization is "path canonicalization," in which file and directory paths on computer file systems or web servers (URL) are canonicalized to enforce access restrictions.

Failure of such canonicalization mechanism can lead to directory traversal or path traversal attacks. The concept of canonicalization is widely applicable and applies equally well to Unicode and XML processing routines.

While expecting UTF-8 encoded characters, the application fails to sanitize and transform input supplied on the form in UTF-7 coding, leading to a cross-site scripting attack. Applications that are internationalized need to support multiple languages that cannot be represented using common ISO-8859-1 (Latin-1) character encoding. Languages such as Chinese and Japanese use thousands of characters and are therefore represented using variable-width encoding schemes. Improperly handled mapping and encoding of such international characters can also lead to canonicalization attacks.[10] Based on input and output handling requirements, applications should identify acceptable character sets and implement custom sanitization routines to process and transform data specific to their needs.

7.6 Common Examples of Attacks Due to Improper Input Handling

Below are classes of some common ways people exploit vulnerabilities caused by improper or absent input validation.

7.6.1 Buffer Overflow

A buffer overflow may occur when the length of the source variable input is not validated before being copied to the destination variable that's not set to accommodate it. The weakness is exploited when the size of "input" (source) exceeds the size of the destination, causing an overflow of the destination variable's address in memory. Sometime a buffer overflow (or overrun) error can force an application to stop operating and yields information about the error that can help an attacker formulate more effective future attacks that will succeed.

7.6.2 OS Commanding

OS commanding (command injection) is an attack technique used for unauthorized execution of operating system commands. Improperly handled input from the user is one of the common weaknesses that can be exploited to run unauthorized commands. Consider a web application exposing a function showInfo() that accepts parameters "name" and "template" from the user and opens a file based on this input

Here's an example:

```
http://example/cgi-bin/showInfo.pl?name=John&template=tmp1.txt
```

As a result of improper or nonexistent input checking, by changing the template parameter value, an attacker can trick the web application into executing the command /bin/ls or open arbitrary files.

Here's the attack example:

```
http://example/cgi-bin/showInfo.pl?name=John&template=/bin/ls|
```

7.7 Best Practices in Validating Input Data

There are several techniques for validating input data, and each one has varying levels of security, with the better ones following the principle of *use a positive security model*, as illustrated in Figure 7.2 below.

Figure 7.2   Input Validation Techniques

7.7.1 Exact Match Validation

For exact match validation, the following elements are in play:

- Data is validated against a list of explicit known values.
- Requires the definition of all possible values that are considered valid input. For example, a choice-based answer: "Yes" and "No."
- Provides the *strongest level of protection* against malicious data, because it limits the attacker to choosing only between the accepted values.
- May not be feasible when a large number of possible good values are expected—for example, generic fields such as name or address.

7.7.2 Exact Match Validation Example

The following two code snippets demonstrate how to validate a variable named *gender* against two known values:

Java example:

```
static boolean validateGender(String gender) {
if(gender.equals("Female"))
     return true;
else if(gender.equals("Male"))
     return true;
else
     return false;
}
```

.NET example:

```
static bool validateGender(String gender) {
if(gender.equals("Female"))
     return true;
else if(gender.equals("Male"))
     return true;
else
     return false;
}
```

7.7.3 Known Good Validation

Known good validation is based on:

- *Whitelist* validation
- Data is validated against a list of allowable characters
- Requires the definition of all characters that are accepted as valid input
- Typically implemented using regular expressions (regex) to match known good data patterns

The following code snippets demonstrate how to validate a variable against a regular expression representing the proper expected data format (10 alphanumeric characters):

Java example:

```
import java.util.regex.*;
static boolean validateUserFormat(String userName){
boolean isValid = false; //Fail by default
try{
// Verify that the UserName is 10 character alphanumeric
if (Pattern.matches("^[A-Za-z0-9]{10}$", userName))
        isValid=true;
}catch(PatternSyntaxException e){
        System.out.println(e.getDescription());
}
return isValid;
```

.NET example:

```
using System.Text.RegularExpressions;
static bool validateUserFormat(String userName){
    bool isValid = false; //Fail by default
    // Verify that the UserName is 1-10 character alphanumeric
    isValid = Regex.IsMatch(userName, @"^[A-Za-z0-9]{10}$");
    return isValid;
}
```

7.7.4 Known Bad Validation

For known bad validation, you'll find:

- *Blacklist* validation (think in term of signatures for previously identified malware and viruses).
- Data is validated against a list of characters that are deemed to be unacceptable.
- Requires the definition of all characters that are considered dangerous to the application.
- Useful for preventing specific characters from being accepted by the application.
- Highly susceptible to evasion using various forms of character encoding.
- Is the *weakest method* of validation against malicious data.

The following code snippets demonstrate how to Validate a variable against a regular expression of known bad input strings :

Java example:

```
import java.util.regex.*;
static boolean checkMessage(string messageText) {
boolean isValid = false; //Fail by default
try{
Pattern P = Pattern.compile("<|>", Pattern.CASE _ INSENSITIVE |
Pattern.MULTILINE);
Matcher M = p.matcher(messageText);
if (!M.find())
    isValid = true;
}catch(Exception e){
    System.out.println(e.toString());
}
return isValid;
}
```

.NET example:

```
using System.Text.RegularExpressions;
static boolean checkMessage(string messageText){
    bool isValid = false; //Fail by default
    // Verify input doesn't contain any <, >
    isValid = !Regex.IsMatch(messageText, @"[><]");
    return isValid;
}
```

7.7.5 Handling Bad Input

Once you detect bad input using any of the above techniques, there are a couple of ways to handle them, again with varying levels of security, as illustrated in Figure 7.3.

Figure 7.3   Handling Bad Input

- **Escaping bad input:** The application attempts to fix the bad input data by encoding the malicious data in a "safe" format.
- **Rejecting bad input:** The application rejects (discards) the input data and displays an error message to the user
  - Rejecting bad input is **always considered better** than escaping.

Detailing all the other specifics on how to remediate the vulnerabilities in the OWASP Top 10 is beyond the scope or intent of this book—there are plenty of secure programming books on the market specific for popular languages—but it's important to understand the fundamental problem and resolutions for unsanitized and unvalidiated inputs that address several of the injection-related Top 10 vulnerabilities. Because languages and platforms are changing all the time, refer to language-specific guidance you can find for the programming platforms in use at your organization.

7.8 OWASP's Secure Coding Practices

A handy *Secure Coding Practices (SCP) Quick Reference Guide*[11] from OWASP is a technology-agnostic set of general software security coding practices in a comprehensive checklist format that can be integrated into the development lifecycle. It contains 214 entries on all aspects of programming, communications, and server configurations related to application security. The focus is on secure coding requirements, rather than on vulnerabilities and exploits. It includes an introduction to software security principles and a glossary of key terms. The SCP is designed to serve as a secure coding kick-start and easy reference to help development teams quickly understand secure coding practices.

The SCP is organized as follows:

- Table of contents
- Introduction
- Software Security Principles Overview
- Secure Coding Practices Checklist
- Links to useful resources
- Glossary of important terminology

7.9 Summary

Chapter 7 covered the importance of secure application development and programming best practices. We examined some of the most pernicious programming issues—injection attacks—and recommended a number of defensive programming techniques to protect applications from those attacks.

In Chapter 8, we turn the attention to security testing activities based on static code analysis. And in Chapter 9, we'll look at dynamic testing that mimics how an attacker might try to attack your product.

References

1. An Illustrated Guide to the Kaminsky DNS Vulnerability. (2008, August 7). Retrieved from http://unixwiz.net/techtips/iguide-kaminsky-dns-vuln.html
2. The DNS Vulnerability. (n.d.). Retrieved from http://www.schneier.com/blog/archives/2008/07/the_dns_vulnera.html
3. djbdns: Domain Name System Tools. (n.d.). Retrieved from https://cr.yp.to/djbdns.html

4. Frequently Asked Questions (FAQ). (2019, April 29). Retrieved from http://cwe. mitre.org/about/faq.html
5. Category:OWASP Top Ten Project. (n.d.). Retrieved from https://www.owasp.org/ index.php/Top_10
6. The Web Application Security Consortium/Improper Input Handling. (n.d.). Retrieved from http://projects.Webappsec.org/Improper-Input-Handling
7. Burp tools. (n.d.). Retrieved from https://portswigger.net/burp/documentation/ desktop/tools
8. CWE—CWE-20: Improper Input Validation (3.3). (2019, June 20). Retrieved from http://cwe.mitre.org/data/definitions/20.html
9. HTML Standard. (n.d.). Retrieved from http://www.w3.org/TR/html5/forms. html#the-pattern-attribute
10. Canonicalization, locale and Unicode. (n.d.). Retrieved from http://www.owasp. org/index.php/Canoncalization,_locale_and_Unicode
11. OWASP Secure Coding Practices—Quick Reference Guide. (n.d.). Retrieved from https://www.owasp.org/index.php/OWASP_Secure_Coding_Practices_-_Quick _Reference_Guide

Chapter 8

Testing Part 1: Static Code Analysis

At this point in the book, we have examined specific techniques and approaches to developing secure and resilient software under the *shift left* and *build security in* paradigms for a variety of platforms and specialized applications, with a focus on preventing the most common errors and problems that lead to security incidents and data losses.

8.1 Chapter Overview

In Chapter 8 we'll begin exploring how to test the resilience of custom application code and find ways to further improve it. Topics covered here include:

- The true costs of waiting to find and eradicate software flaws
- Manual and automated source code review techniques
- Shifting left with code analysis tools

8.2 Fixing Early versus Fixing Later

A study by Gartner, IBM, and The National Institute of Standards and Technology (NIST)[1] revealed that *"The cost of removing an application security vulnerability during the design/development phase ranges from 30–60 times less than if removed during production operations.*" The key objective of integrating security processes with the software development life cycle (SDLC) is to ensure that we detect and fix security vulnerabilities early (shift left).

Many organizations simply do not know the true costs of finding and fixing software defects, because they do not track or measure that work. If they did, they might be shocked to learn the actual costs of developing software. There are direct and indirect costs to finding and fixing security defects. If a vulnerability is found and exploited in a production application, the brand damage that results cannot be easily measured or repaired.

There are direct costs that we can certainly measure. One of the easiest to measure is the average cost to code a fix:

```
Average cost to code a fix = (number of developer man-days * cost
per man-day) ÷ number of defects fixed
```

Apart from this cost, there are additional costs we need to consider:

- System testing costs
- Implementation costs
- System deployment and operations costs
- Postproduction costs
- Other costs, such as project management, documentation, downtime costs, etc.

These costs can skyrocket when a mission-critical or high-profile application is involved, and changes to it must not interfere or even be seen by customers using the application over the Internet—for instance, an e-banking site.

Instead, it is far more sensible for enterprises to find and fix application software defects before they are released into the production environment. Although threat modeling and design and architecture reviews can help to assure that there are no high-level defects at the design level, security testing ensures that there are no known defects when *implementing* that secure design.

There are several techniques to conducting thorough security testing of an application. They range from simple developer-driven unit tests to highly focused penetration testing by a specialized team of security experts. In this chapter we focus on the former, and Chapter 9 covers the latter.

8.3 Testing Phases

Typical software development testing occurs in multiple iterative phases, with the completion of one signaling the beginning of the next. Each of these phases has room for security and resilience testing activities and is described within each phase:

- Unit testing
- Integration testing
- Quality assurance testing
- User acceptance testing

8.3.1 Unit Testing

Developers drive and conduct unit tests on the code that they write and own. Unit testing is a best practice from an overall code quality perspective and has security advantages. Unit testing helps prevent defects from finding their way into the larger testing phases. Because developers understand their own code better than anyone else, simple unit testing ensures effectiveness of the test.

Developers need to make sure that they also document what they test, because it is very easy to miss a test that is performed by hand. Some of the key issues a developer can find in unit testing include:

- Boundary conditions
  - Integer over/underflows
  - Path length (URL, file)
  - Buffer overflows
- When writing code in the C language and coding their own memory management routines, all arithmetic pertaining to those should be tested as well.

Developers can also conduct direct security testing using *fuzzing* techniques. Fuzzing, in simplest terms, is sending random data to the interfaces that the program uses to determine what, when, and how it might break the software.

Fuzzing is usually done in several iterations (100,000+) and can be made smarter by doing targeted variations in key parts of data structures (length fields, etc.). Fuzzing is an effective test that most developers can perform themselves. It is one of the cheapest, fastest, and most effective ways to identify security bugs, even in organizations that have mature SDLC security and resilience programs.

8.3.2 Manual Source Code Reviews

Manual source code reviews can begin when there is sufficient code from the development process to review. The scope of a source code review is usually limited to finding code-level problems that could potentially result in security vulnerabilities. Code reviews are *not* used to reveal:

- Problems related to business requirements that cannot be implemented securely
- Issues with the selection of a particular technology for the application
- Design issues that might result in vulnerabilities

Source code reviews typically do not worry about the exploitability of vulnerabilities. Findings from the review are treated just like any other defects found by other methods, and they are handled in the same ways. Code reviews are also useful for non-security findings that can affect the overall code quality. Code reviews typically result in the identification of not only security problems but also dead code, redundant code, unnecessary complexity, or any other violation of the best practices that we've covered throughout the book. Each of the findings carries its own priority, which is typically defined in the organization's "bug priority matrix." Bug reports often contain a specific remediation recommendation by the reviewer so that the developer can fix it appropriately.

Manual code reviews are expensive because they involve many manual efforts and often involve security specialists to assist in the review. However, manual reviews have proven their value repeatedly when it comes to accuracy and quality. They also help identify logic vulnerabilities that typically cannot be identified by automated static code analyzers.

Source code reviews are often called "white box" analysis. This is because the reviewer has complete internal knowledge of the design, threat models, and other system documentation for the application. "Black box" analysis, covered in Chapter 9, on the other hand, is performed from an outsider's view of the application, with no access to specifications or knowledge of the application's inner workings. "Gray box" analysis is somewhere in between white box and black box analysis.

The Code Review Process

The code review process begins with the Scrum team making sure that there is enough time and budget allocated in the SDLC to perform these reviews. Tools that are helpful in performing these reviews should be made available to all developers and reviewers.

The code review process consists of four high-level steps, illustrated in Figure 8.1.

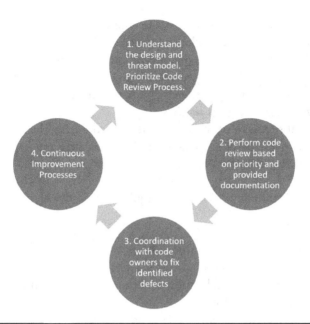

Figure 8.1   Code Review Process

- The first step in the code review process is to understand what the application does (its business purpose), its internal design, and the threat models prepared for the application. This understanding greatly helps in identifying the critical components of the code and assigning priorities to them. The reality is that there is not enough time to review every single line of code in the entire application every time. Therefore, it is vital to understand the most critical components and ensure that they are reviewed completely.
- The second step is to begin reviewing the identified critical components based on their priority. This review can be done either by a different Scrum team who were not originally involved in the application's development or by a team of security experts. Another approach is to use the same Scrum team who built the application to perform peer reviews of each other's code. Regardless of how code reviews are accomplished, it is vital that they cover the most critical components and that both developers and security experts have a chance to see them. All the identified defects should be documented using the enterprise's defect management tool and are assigned the appropriate priority. The reviewers must document these defects along with their recommended fix approaches to make sure they do not creep into final production code.

- The third step of a code review is to coordinate with the application code owners and help them implement the fixes for the problems revealed in the review. These may involve the integration of an existing, reusable security component available to developers (e.g., reusable libraries for Single Sign On or cryptography functions), or it may require simple-to-complex code changes and subsequent reviews.
- The final step is to study the lessons learned during the review cycle and identify areas for improvement. This makes sure the next code review cycle is more effective and efficient.

Some of critical components that require a deep-dive review and analysis follow:

- User authentication and authorization
- Data protection routines
- Code that receives and handles data from untrusted sources
- Data validation routines
- Code involved in handling error conditions
- Use of operating system resources and networks
- Low-level infrastructure code (which does its own memory management)
- Embedded software components
- Use of problematic/deprecated APIs

Because manual analysis is time consuming and expensive, enterprises often implement automated source code analysis tools to complement—not replace—manual reviews.

8.4 Static Source Code Analysis

Few enterprises can afford to conduct a manual code review on every single application every single time. Instead, many rely on automated source code analyzers to help.

Typical software development priorities are schedule, cost, features, and then quality—in most cases, in that order. The pressure from a time-to-market perspective can negatively affect software quality and resilience and sometimes cause the postponement of adding features to the software.

As Phillip Crosby said, "Quality is free,"[2] and this is most true of the software development process. However, managers in organizations that do software development often believe otherwise: they appear to think that a focus on software quality increases costs and delays projects. Studies of software quality (not necessarily software security) have consistently proven this belief wrong. Organizations with a mature SDLC process usually face little extra overhead because attention to software quality and resilience, and the corresponding cost savings from process improvements, *far exceed* the cost of added developer activities.

Static application security testing (SAST) supports the secure development of programs in an organization by finding and listing the potential security bugs in the code base; this is one of the most powerful processes in implementing a shift left model. SAST tools offer a wide variety of views/reports and trends on the security posture of the code base and can be used as an effective mechanism to collect metrics that indicate the progress and maturity of the software security activities. Source code analyzers operate relatively quickly compared to the several thousands of man-hours needed to complete the analysis if it were done manually. Automated tools also provide risk rankings for each vulnerability, which helps the organization to prioritize its remediation strategies.

Most important, automated code analyzers help an organization uncover defects earlier in the SDLC, enabling the kinds of cost and reputation savings we discussed earlier in this chapter. Here are a number of other tangible and intangible benefits come that from using SAST:

- Brand protection from reduced risks from potential security exploits.
- Improvement in delivery of secure and dependable application software solutions.
- Reduction in the cost of remediation by addressing security vulnerabilities earlier in the development life cycle (compared to expensive post-production fixes).
- Assurance to business owners/partners and auditors/regulators about effectiveness of security controls.
- Compliance with standards and internal/external audit requirements.
- Easier security automation in the software development lifecycle.
- Improved developer skills through regular use of the tool helps to ensure ongoing quality improvements in custom-built software.
- Effective tool to collect and track software security metrics.

8.5 Automated Reviews Compared with Manual Reviews

Although SAST tools are strong at performing with low incremental costs, are good at catching the typical low-hanging fruit, have an ability to scale to several thousands of lines of code, and are good at performing repetitive tasks quickly, they also have a few drawbacks.

- Automated tools sometimes report a high number of false positives. Sometimes it will take an organization several months to fine tune the tool to reduce these false positives, but some level of noise will always remain in the findings.
- Source code analyzers are poor at detecting business logic flaws.
- Some of the other types of attacks that automated analysis cannot detect are complex information leakage, design flaws, subjective vulnerabilities such as cross-site request forgery, sophisticated race conditions, and multistep-process attacks.

We'll cover running times as a drawback later in this chapter.

8.6 Peeking Inside SAST Tools

It's risky to deploy SAST tools before the workforce is prepared to incorporate their use into the Scrum process, because there's little point in asking Scrum teams who are unprepared to use the scanners regularly and react to the scan results to use them. On the other hand, such deployments happen all the time. When this happens, the following situation becomes commonplace:

- Applications are selected for scanning, and SAST scans are run.
- Reports of the scan results are prepared and shared with the team responsible for the application.
- Developers don't understand what the reports are telling them and settle into bewilderment that leads to inaction or analysis paralysis.
- When developers do react, it's often with incredulous disbelief that their program is capable of being defective and the security team must be wrong or crazy or is picking on them.
- Appsec architects responsible for this new processing are left holding the ever-growing bag of software defects that cannot be addressed properly and waits while management escalations resolve what's now become a human–factors-based incident for managers in multiple areas to address.

This situation plays out everywhere whenever a workforce is unprepared for new tools and is being required to do something they're unprepared to do. This results in ill regard by developers for the security team, the management team, and the entire SDLC process. Always remember, appsec is a people—not a technical—issue.

The good news is there's a better way.

Treating SAST as a developer-oriented and developer-based tool usually transforms the process from a bad implementation to a helpful enrichment of the SDLC. The best first step to making that happen is, once again, education. AppSec practitioners should not make the mistake of thinking that SAST tools were developed for security professionals. They were mostly written *by* developers *for* developers to help resolve the scourge of bad software. SAST tools offer plenty to the security team, but their primary purpose is to help developers become better developers.

Teaching people what SAST is all about, how SAST tools work, and how the scanner data is useful for improving software quality fortifies the skills that developers need to meet the acceptance criteria for the user stories they're working on.

According to Gartner,[3] SAST is a set of technologies designed to analyze application code, byte code, and binaries for coding and design conditions that are indicative of security vulnerabilities. SAST solutions analyze an application from the "inside out" in a nonrunning state.

Without getting into the heavy computer science behind SAST tools, suffice it to say that a SAST tool suite consists of a scanning engine, an interface to process scan results, special processing to identify security issues in Open Source and third-party code libraries, and may include dynamic testing and other appsec-related components within the suite. Some tools are run on premises and others are offered as SaaS-based cloud services. Some tools are free for the taking from Open Source projects, whereas others cost millions of dollars, depending on your application portfolio.

In essence, the SAST engine receives a copy of the *compiled* modules for the application and begins a reverse-engineering process that builds a database to represent the application and its control and data flows. The engine then runs queries against the database to trace how variables and control (branching) flows through the application.

The basic premise is this:

When a tainted variable reaches a sink, a security vulnerability is declared.

A better understanding of this model requires knowing a few key terms:

Trust Boundary (security perimeter). In the case of SAST, *only* the packaged application binaries are considered within the trust boundary. Everything outside this perimeter is explicitly distrusted.

Source. The point of entry of data at which variables are set with values that come from outside the trust boundary.

Sink. The point of exit for data at which variables are used in computing processes or are sent to a file, a database, a screen, or a command or are subsequently used in another external process.

Taint. The condition ascribed to every variable that's found at a source. *Tainted* is the label that's affixed to that variable as data comes in and control flow proceeds. Any data that enters the trust boundary is tagged as tainted as the implementation of explicit distrust.

Vulnerability. The condition in which a variable that still is tagged as tainted reaches a sink with no intervening function that "removes" the taint.

Cleanser or Taint Removal. A software routine that the scanner recognizes as a viable function that removes the taint tag when the variable is output from the process. It can be a data validation routine (white list) or a built-in framework service, such as XSS Prevention suite in Microsoft's .NET.

Taint Propagation. This happens when another variable is set to the value of a variable that's still tagged as tainted. This new variable is also tagged as tainted, as is any other variable that uses it in a calculation or process. One tainted variable can propagate throughout the application, and when any of those variables reach a sink, a vulnerability is declared.

Figure 8.2 shows a diagram of the model used for SAST.

Once the database that the scanning engine produces for analysis is ready, a series of queries are run on it, looking for data flows and control flows as variables move from source to sink as they're processed in the trust boundary. If the scanner detects that the variable has flowed through a taint removal or cleansing function, the taint tag for that variable is removed. If a variable reaches a sink with the tainted tag still attached, a vulnerability of some sort is declared.

The process occurring at the sink determines the exact vulnerability. If the sink is a SQL statement that's constructed using a tainted variable, SQL injection is reported. If the variable is reflected to another web page or service, cross-site scripting (XSS) is reported. If the variable is used in a command string, command injection is reported, and so forth, as shown in Figure 8.3. In this case, a cleansing function was invoked for var2, which then shows as clean with the taint tag removed. In the case where var2 was not cleansed, the reported vulnerability would be XSS.

Scanners typically report the CWE™ number of the weakness it finds, along with the severity of the weakness (critical, high, medium, low, informational). When the final scanning is done, a report is produced, and the submitter of it is notified. The report will contain a score or an outcome—pass, conditional pass, fail. This process is shown in Figure 8.3 data and control flow analysis in SAST.

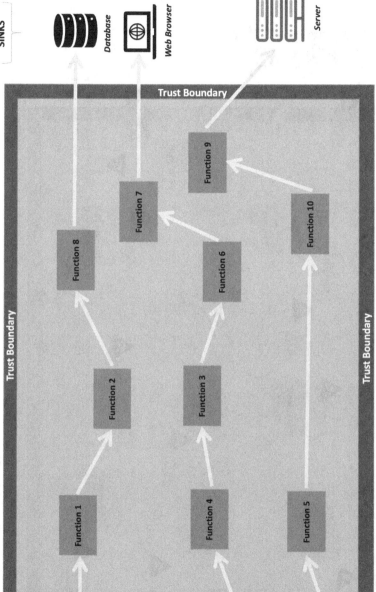

Figure 8.2 SAST Model of Environment under Analysis

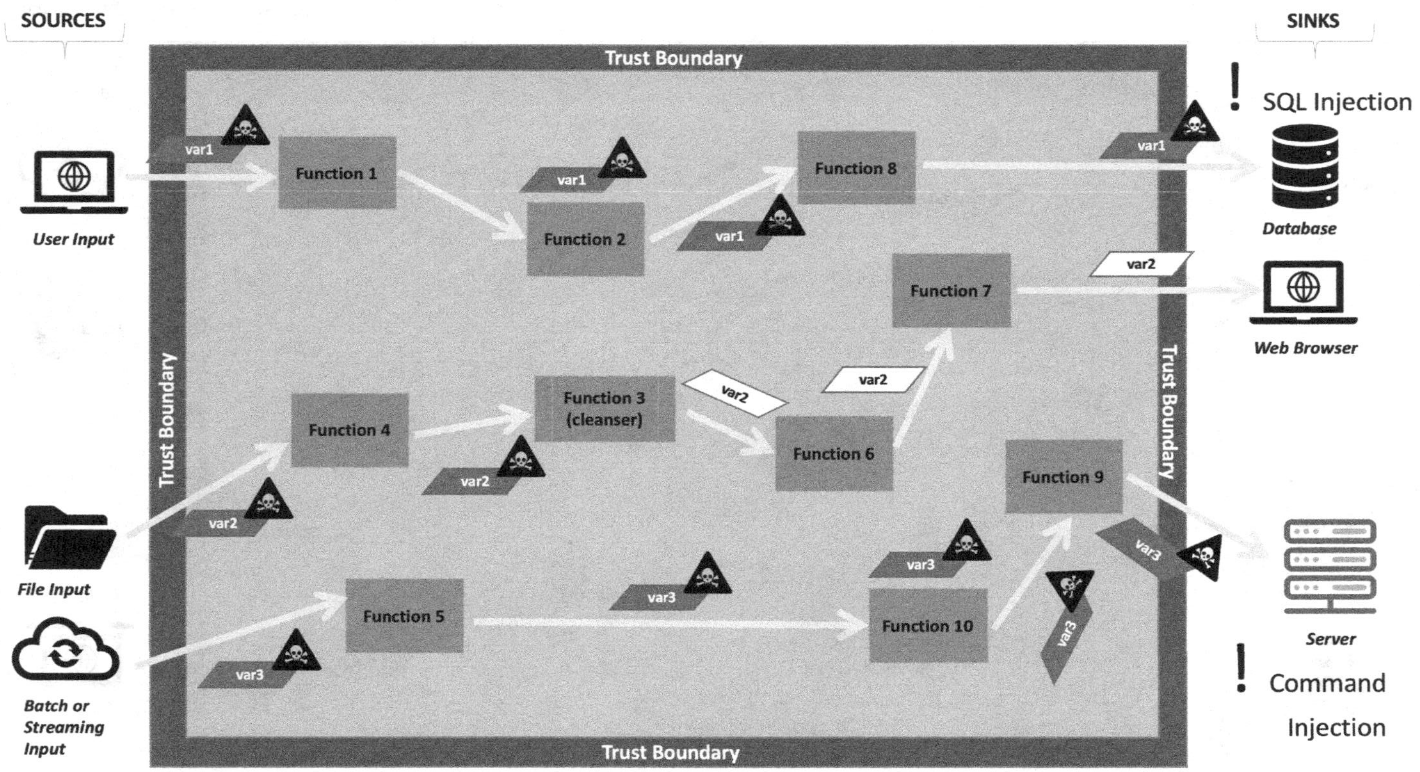

Figure 8.3 Finding Vulnerabilities Using SAST

8.7 SAST Policies

Completed scans are the point at which the security team and the Scrum team intersect; the outcome and score of the scan is based on a policy for scanning that's established by the security team. One such policy might require a *fail* if there are any *critical* or *high* vulnerabilities found in the scan. Another policy might require a *failure* if there are any *critical, high,* and some subset of *medium-*level defects. These choices should be made deliberatively between the security and development teams management.

It's also possible to opt for a lighter-weight approach in which only certain vulnerabilities would cause a *fail* result. For example, a firm might opt to start with SQL injection and one or two other CWEs to get the ball rolling, then ease the entry into full-bore use. Another option is to make sure that there are no OWASP Top 10 vulnerabilities present. This can be accomplished by filtering out other CWEs not in the Top 10 and using that to set the policy for the scanner outcomes.

Using SAST tools and building a process around it to help ensure compliance to organizational requirements for software security, while working hand in hand with Scrum teams across the enterprise, is extremely challenging and time consuming. Here's where the security team should treat their roles as stewards or shepherds to guide Scrum teams into using the processing and tools correctly, while Scrum team members begin to take personal responsibility to bake in their new-found defensive programming skills. Forcing the use of these tools too early or without the process and support structures in place is a surefire pathway to failure. Again, and again, software security is a people issue, so any solution needs to fit within the DNA of how Scrum teams conduct their work.

8.8 Using SAST in Development Sprints

Shifting left and building security in can be visibly implemented at the moment developers save the work they're doing within their integrated development environment (IDE). Today's SAST tools often include what you can think of as a *security spell checker.* These tools come as plug-ins to the IDE and are invoked automatically when some code is saved by the developer. Once it's done, the checker will highlight segments of code and provide an explanation of what it found, why it's a problem, and what to do about it, such as the use of insecure functions or data found at a source that's not sanitized. A product in this family from Veracode is called Greenlight,[4] and one from Synopsys is called SecureAssist.[5] Remember, a defect that's made, caught, and eliminated at the point it's introduced is a defect that won't appear in a feature branch.

These tools are not perfect, and they can't see the entire application or even enough of it to substitute for running a complete scan. Instead, we recommend what's called *sandbox scanning*. Typically, scanners are set up for each application that needs scanning. Scans run in the policy area of the tool are collected and reported as *official* scans, which often appear in dashboards and reports from the tool that aggregate results. Application-specific work areas are separate from other application work areas and are flexible, so you can set up scanning to run automatically, based on some schedule for the frequency of release and deployment. You can also set up sandboxes for scanning that you don't want reported as Policy Scans. These sandboxes should be used regularly by the Scrum team, and defects should be removed as quickly as is practical. Once a *clean scan* (according to policy) is attained, it's possible to *promote* that scan as a *policy* or *gated* scan, as proof of meeting acceptance criteria or Definition of Done.

This raises another important issue: not all scanner-reported defects are equal. Some are riskier to leave untreated than others, whereas others may need to wait on the back burner until riskier issues are addressed.

Furthermore, it's possible to *rationalize* that some reported vulnerabilities cannot be exploited (and are a reduced risk) because of some controls outside the trust boundary that prevent tainted data from entering the boundary. Other rationalization may involve declaring that an internal function serves as a cleanser, but the scanner does not recognize it as an established cleanser.

It's also possible that there's a routine—for example, in batch processing—in which data is previously *cleansed or purified* because several downstream applications need this level of data purification. If there is evidence that this is indeed true and that the process is working as expected, SAST tools often let you indicate that the vulnerability is *mitigated* (not remediated) because of external factors. Typically, a developer or Scrum team security champion will propose this mitigation inside the scanner triage view and let the security team know a *mitigation proposal* is ready for review for the specific application. The security team will meet with the proposer and discuss the situation. If the security staff is convinced, they can approve the proposal, and the vulnerability will be tagged as *mitigated*. These mitigated vulnerabilities improve the overall outcome for the scan, but remain on the scan history for its lifetime.

For an example of how this process could work, MITRE produced a guide called "Monster Mitigations"[6] that's connected to the CWE Top 25 Most Dangerous Programming Errors.[7] These monster mitigations are intended to reduce the severity or impact of reported vulnerabilities to help with practical risk management of appsec concerns. You can use this guidance to help development teams understand how to propose mitigations when the situation is right for them. These can also be reused across teams and scans as experience with the SAST tool is gained.

Cleansers and Custom Cleansers

SAST products such as Veracode[8] publish a list of standardized framework-level and language-specific functions for scanner users that are recognized as cleansers. Figure 8.4 shows an example of just a few Veracode-recognized cleansers and indicates which CWEs the cleanser addresses:

This list runs for pages and pages and includes all supported cleansing functions for .NET, Java, C, Classic ASP, ColdFusion, Perl, PHP, and Ruby. Use these in your own code as data validation, sanitization, or cleansing functions, and you'll quickly reduce the occurrence of vulnerabilities in your scans.

Sometimes, a scanning tool will permit you to identify internally developed functions and routines that work as cleansing functions. You can configure the scanner to recognize these as custom cleansers.

Developers often write their own libraries and functions to address common application security problems. Custom cleansers[9] allow a security architect to mark certain functions in the application code as "trusted" ways to make user data safe for use, reducing the number of findings that the development team has to review. When the scanner detects their use, it can automatically do one of two things with it, based on your policy for custom cleansers.

- It can create an automatic mitigation proposal that someone needs to review and approve.
- It can create an automatic mitigation proposal that is automatically approved.

By leaving these vulnerabilities tagged as mitigated, audit teams and governance teams can find the evidence on how they're used and permit security teams to find and treat uses of custom cleansers, should one be discovered as no longer effective in taint removal or exploitation prevention.

8.9 Software Composition Analysis (SCA)

Modern commercial SAST products and many Open Source SAST projects offer an additional resource that helps with the secure use of external components and libraries for code development, called Software Composition Analysis, or SCA.

In a 2018 article entitled, "The percentage of open source code in proprietary apps is rising,"[10] the author notes:

Supported Java Cleansing Functions

Function	Flaw Class
android.net.Uri.encode	CWE 80, 93, 117 and 113
com.google.gwt.safehtml.shared.SafeHtmlUtils.htmlEscape	CWE 80, 93, 117 and 113
com.google.gwt.safehtml.shared.SafeHtmlUtils.htmlEscapeAllowEntities	CWE 80, 93, 117 and 113
com.google.gwt.safehtml.shared.SafeHtmlUtils.fromString	CWE 80, 93, 117 and 113
com.liferay.portal.kernel.util.HtmlUtil.escapeAttribute	CWE 80, 93, 117 and 113
com.liferay.portal.kernel.util.HtmlUtil.escape	CWE 80, 93, 117 and 113
com.liferay.portal.kernel.util.HtmlUtil.escapeCSS	CWE 80, 93, 117 and 113
com.liferay.portal.kernel.util.HtmlUtil.escapeREF	CWE 80, 93, 117 and 113
com.liferay.portal.kernel.util.HtmlUtil.escapeJS	CWE 80, 93, 117 and 113
com.liferay.portal.kernel.util.HtmlUtil.escapeURL	CWE 80, 93, 117 and 113
com.liferay.portal.kernel.util.HtmlUtil.escapeXPath	CWE 80, 93, 117 and 113
com.liferay.portal.kernel.util.HtmlUtil.escapeXPathAttribute	CWE 80, 93, 117 and 113
com.oreilly.servlet.Base64encoder.Encode	CWE 80, 93, 117 and 113
java.net.URLencoder.Encode	CWE 80, 93, 117 and 113
org.tuckey.web.filters.validation.utils.StringEscapeUtils.escapeHtml	CWE 80

Figure 8.4 Some Sample Veracode-Recognized Cleansers

"Compiled after examining the findings from the anonymized data of over 1,100 commercial codebases audited in 2017 by the Black Duck On-Demand audit services group, the report revealed that:

- 96 percent of the scanned applications contain open source components, with an average 257 components per application, and that
- The average percentage of open source in the codebases of the applications scanned grew from 36% last year to 57%, suggesting that a large number of applications now contain much more open source than proprietary code."

They also revealed from the study that 78 percent of the codebases examined contained at least one vulnerability, with an average 64 vulnerabilities per codebase.

Vulnerabilities on these components are maintained in a separate dictionary from the MITRE Corporation called Common Vulnerabilities and Exposures, or CVE®.[11] CVE is a collection of the known or reported vulnerabilities in purchased, commercial off-the-shelf (COTS) products, and free-for-the-taking Open Source projects found in repositories such as GitHub and others. CVE is a list of entries, each containing an identification number, a description, and at least one public reference for publicly known cybersecurity vulnerabilities. CVE is a companion to the CWE but applies to commercial and freely available public sources or reusable code.

SCA scans are run when any scan is run. The ability to view the results of these depends on your license(s) for using the scanner. When SCA is available, any of the vulnerabilities that are found on the specific versions of open source components in the trust boundary are reported on the scanner's scan report facilities. It will list the version of the vulnerable library, including which vulnerabilities from CVE are reported on it, and provides some assistance on updating the library to a version that's not reported as vulnerable (if one exists). These results, along with custom code scan results, are available to the Scrum team developers and security champion, where they can be properly triaged and set up for next steps to remediate or mitigate the threats.

SAST Running Times

You'll find that SAST tools, which are getting better all the time, have a drawback that affects how they're used. Basically, the larger the application, the longer it takes for a scan to run and produce results. Sometimes they'll run for hours, or even days. As you appreciate the complexity of the work that scanners perform, you can understand that they need the time to run for complete analysis. *Never force a SAST scan activity into any development process that runs serially or synchronously.* You don't want people waiting around for the scan before they can do their jobs. After you have a good idea on how long your application takes to scan, you can work this in so other sprint work can proceed asynchronously, and the sprint planners can plan future time to process the scans.

Provided you have *no expectation* that a SAST tool preforming a comprehensive analysis runs in a few seconds or a few minutes, you'll be prepared to help the Scrum team automate the tasks of scanning and preparing for the tasks of handling the outcomes.

8.10 SAST is NOT for the Faint of Heart!

As you're learning, using SAST tools draws on the need to apply *people, process, and technology* for effective use that helps reduce the release of defective software. These needs are not lightweight or trivial—they require close attention by the security team so they won't impose undue requirements on the Scrum team's time or budgets. Scrum team members will be expected to use and consume the scan results, so they'll need to work those efforts into sprint activities, and both teams need to work together to develop common processes that enable policy setting, mitigation reviews and approvals, and planning on how to treat medium-level flaws that will be included as the policies get tighter and program maturity increases.

Adopters of SAST tools should be prepared to staff the function inside Scrum teams, nominate a person who can best represent the application to work with the security team (security champions), and provide enough people on the security teams to help with training developers on secure development practices and how to use the SAST tool in the way it's intended for use.

Plan your implementation deliberately, and resist the urge to crack down on compliance with the scan results before your processes and constituents are prepared. Pick a team or two (not a mission-critical application team, though!) and experiment with the tool and internal processes. As you learn more about how the tool works and how your processes really work, you'll be able to integrate it into Agile workflows, similar to how NFRs get integrated—with agility and practicality.

8.11 Commercial and Free SAST Tools

There are dozens of SAST tools out there, some for the taking, others for commercial licensing. Your environment should dictate which is the best tool to use and what kinds of flexibility and robustness you need. One good way to help determine this is a bake-off—using your Scrum teams and your security teams working together to develop solutions. Pick a few to evaluate, and gather your stakeholders to learn their needs for appsec and how SAST can contribute to those efforts.

For a listing of some common commercial and open source SAST tools, see Appendix B.

8.12 Summary

In Chapter 8, we explored the overall landscape for software testing and the areas within it. You saw a multi-step process for testing, beginning with the first elements of source code, all the way through comprehensive static code analysis using complex SAST tools.

As you are continuing to see, testing for security and resilience requires comprehensive tools and techniques along with skilled personnel who can collect and analyze software from a number of points of view. The principle of "defense in depth" is equally applicable in the testing phases of the SDLC, because they are within the design and development phases. There is no single tool or technique that can uncover all security-related problems or issues.

In Chapter 9, we'll turn our attention to testing using dynamic and external methods to learn how the program behaves as it's running.

References

1. Control–SA-11–DEVELOPER SECURITY TESTING AND EVALUATION. (n.d.). Retrieved from https://nvd.nist.gov/800-53/Rev4/control/SA-11
2. Crosby, P. B. (1996). *Quality Is Still Free: Making Quality Certain in Uncertain Times*. New York, NY: McGraw-Hill Companies.
3. Static Application Security Testing (SAST). (2019, April 12). Retrieved from https://www.gartner.com/it-glossary/static-application-security-testing-sast/
4. Greenlight Product Page. (2019, April 25). Retrieved from https://www.veracode.com/products/greenlight
5. SecureAssist Overview & Datasheet. (2019, April 15). Retrieved from https://www.synopsys.com/software-integrity/resources/datasheets/secureassist.html
6. 2011 CWE/SANS Top 25: Monster Mitigations. (2011, June 27). Retrieved from https://cwe.mitre.org/top25/mitigations.html
7. CWE/SANS Top 25 Archive. (2019, June 20). Retrieved from https://cwe.mitre.org/top25/archive/index.html

8. Veracode. (n.d.). Supported Cleansing Functions. Retrieved August 9, 2019, from https://help.veracode.com/reader/DGHxSJy3Gn3gtuSIN2jkRQ/y52kZojXR27 Y8XY51KtvvA

9. Streamlining Scan Results: Introducing Veracode Custom Cleansers. (2017, December 7). Retrieved from https://www.veracode.com/blog/managing-appsec/ streamlining-scan-results-introducing-veracode-custom-cleansers

10. The Percentage of Open Source Code in Proprietary Apps Is Rising. (2018, May 22). Retrieved from https://www.helpnetsecurity.com/2018/05/22/open-source-code-security-risk/

11. CVE. Common Vulnerabilities and Exposures (CVE). (n.d.). Retrieved from https://cve.mitre.org/

Chapter 9

Testing Part 2: Penetration Testing/Dynamic Analysis/IAST/RASP

In Chapter 8 we looked at a number of ways to conduct static testing on custom-developed applications when design documentation and source code are available to the testing teams and security experts. In this chapter we shift the focus to dynamic application security testing (DAST), along with some runtime security controls that serve as additional layers of Defense in Depth.

9.1 Chapter Overview

In Chapter 9 we'll look at the other side of the coin for application testing—DAST—that actively attacks a running application. You need both SAST and DAST for a 360-degree view of how your application is built and how it behaves.

DAST tools are a form of penetration testing or Black Box testing, in that testers don't need to possess the knowledge about the application, its design, structure, or requirements. On the other hand, DAST tools are rather potent as attack tools, so their use should be well controlled and well understood.

9.2 Penetration (Pen) Testing

Penetration testing (pen testing) involves actively attacking and analyzing the behavior of a deployed application or network devices. Penetration testing is performed from the perspective of an outside attacker (one who has no inside knowledge of the application) and involves exploiting identified vulnerabilities to break the system or gain access to unauthorized information. The intent of a penetration test is not only to identify potential vulnerabilities but also to determine exploitability of an attack and the degree of business impact of a successful exploit.

Black box testing is the set of activities that occurs during the pre-deployment test phase or on a periodic basis after a system has been deployed. Security experts and skilled QA Testers perform this testing with the help of automated tools and/or manual penetration testing. Many organizations carry out black box tests to comply with regulatory requirements, protect their customers' confidential and sensitive information, and protect the organization's brand and reputation.

A manual penetration test involves humans actually attacking the system by sending malicious requests and carefully inspecting every single response. They carry out the testing *by hand*, with or without the help of penetration testing software, but they do not rely exclusively on the automated testing tool to perform all the work. The most significant advantage of manual penetration testing is the ability to discover business logic vulnerabilities. The obvious drawback is that it is costly and time-consuming, since it requires humans with specialized skills to perform.

Pen testing or black box scanners can take quite a while to completely analyze a complex or large application. Days for them to complete is not unusual, so it's important to be careful when determining where in the SDLC to use these scanners. Like SAST products, you don't want people waiting around for results until they can perform their jobs.

9.3 Open Source Security Testing Methodology Manual (OSSTMM)

A useful guide to help with planning how to conduct pen testing is the Open Source Security Testing Methodology Manual (OSSTMM)[1] as a peer-reviewed methodology for performing security tests and metrics. OSSTMM test cases are divided into five channels (sections) which collectively test:

- Information and data controls
- Personnel security awareness levels

- Fraud and social engineering control levels
- Computer and telecommunications networks
- Wireless devices, mobile devices
- Physical security access controls, security processes, and physical locations such as buildings, perimeters, and military bases

The Institute for Security and Open Methodologies (ISECOM) began with the release of the OSSTMM in the early 2000s. Many researchers from various fields contributed to the effort in developing an open document to help appsec professionals to set up and operate an effective Pen Testing program.

ISECOM also publishes a free, regularly updated Open Source Cybersecurity Playbook for appsec professionals to use, with 27 pages of practical advice and tactics. It's intended to help you to lay out a detailed game plan you can use to take control of your security and close your gaps. You can get a copy of OSSTMM and the Playbook from the ISECOM Web site.[2]

9.4 OWASP's ASVS

Another important guide for Pen Testing planning is the OWASP Application Security Verification Standard 4.0,[3] or ASVS. The latest edition of ASVS was released to the public in March 2019. The ASVS Project provides a basis for testing Web application technical security controls and provides developers with a list of requirements for secure development.

The primary aim of the OWASP Application Security Verification Standard (ASVS) Project is to normalize the range in the coverage and level of rigor available in the market when performing Web application security verification using a commercially workable open standard. The standard provides a basis for testing application technical security controls, as well as any technical security controls in the environment, that are relied on to protect against vulnerabilities such as Cross-Site Scripting (XSS) and SQL injection. This standard can be used to establish a level of confidence in the security of Web applications. The requirements were developed with the following objectives in mind:

- As a metric—Provide application developers and application owners with a yardstick with which to assess the degree of trust that can be placed in their Web applications
- As guidance—Provide guidance to security control developers as to what to build into security controls in order to satisfy application security requirements
- During procurement—Provide a basis for specifying application security verification requirements in contracts.

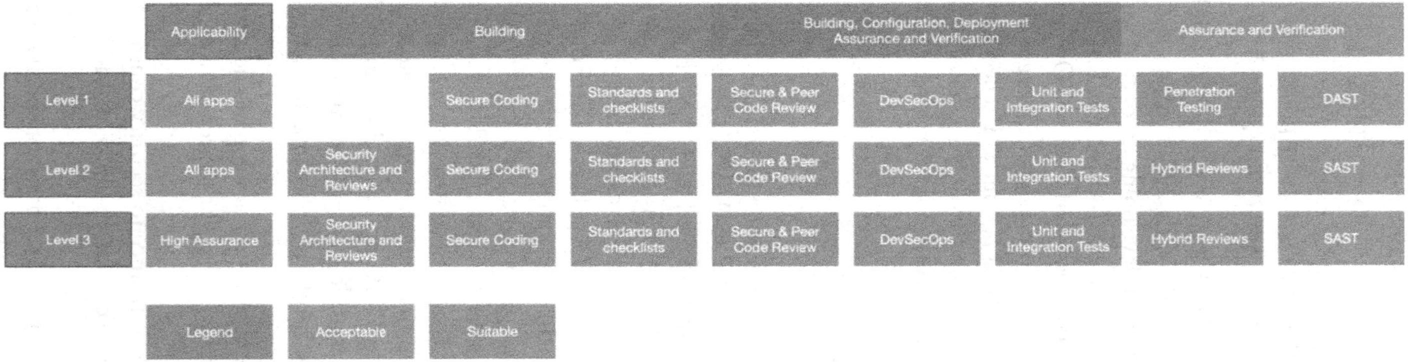

Figure 9.1 ASVS Version 4 Levels

	Applicability	Building				Building, Configuration, Deployment Assurance and Verification		Assurance and Verification	
Level 1	All apps		Secure Coding	Standards and checklists	Secure & Peer Code Review	DevSecOps	Unit and Integration Tests	Penetration Testing	DAST
Level 2	All apps	Security Architecture and Reviews	Secure Coding	Standards and checklists	Secure & Peer Code Review	DevSecOps	Unit and Integration Tests	Hybrid Reviews	SAST
Level 3	High Assurance	Security Architecture and Reviews	Secure Coding	Standards and checklists	Secure & Peer Code Review	DevSecOps	Unit and Integration Tests	Hybrid Reviews	SAST

Legend: Acceptable | Suitable

The Application Security Verification Standard defines three security verification levels, with each level increasing in depth.

- ASVS Level 1 is for low assurance levels, and is completely penetration testable
- ASVS Level 2 is for applications that contain sensitive data, which requires protection and is the recommended level for most apps
- ASVS Level 3 is for the most critical applications—applications that perform high value transactions, contain sensitive medical data, or any application that requires the highest level of trust.

Figure 9.1 below shows the context of the ASVS and its three levels.

One of the best ways to use the Application Security Verification Standard is as a blueprint to create or supplement a Secure Coding Checklist specific to your application, platform, or organization. Tailoring the ASVS to your acceptance criteria will increase the focus on the security NFRs that are most important to your projects and environments.

9.5 Penetration Testing Tools

The "Swiss Army knife" of a hacker usually has several tools, from port scanners to Web application proxies like the one we looked at in Chapter 6. Most all of the Open Source pen testing tools come bundled within the free Kali Linux distribution from Offensive Security. It has tools for application level attacks, network level attacks, and everything in between. Kali Linux is part of the standard toolbox for most professional pen testers. It's a handy tool for people starting on the path to hacking custom-developed applications since everything a hacker needs are there in one place.

Because of the risks when conducting Pen Testing, it's best to perform that testing in the QA Environment. Applications running in Production may be vulnerable and if those vulnerabilities are exploited, the application may stop running or cause the loss of real data.

9.6 Automated Pen Testing with Black Box Scanners

Similar to the automated analysis of source code (SAST), you can carry out automated black box penetration testing. There are lots of misconceptions related to DAST products, including:

- DAST is a point-and-shoot solution.
- DAST can comprehensively cover an entire application by following links on the data collection pages.
- DAST is useful for non-Web applications.

None of these statements are true.

DAST tools need to be "taught" how to follow the logic and flow and data entry, in the context of the business use of the application. For example, an E-commerce application with a catalog, shopping cart, and checkout process can become rather complex rather quickly. Testers who are making sure that the application is working properly in a business context often run and record these tests and make sure that the test data supports the ability to test the application from start to finish. For example, if a product is selected from the catalog, but there's no inventory of it available, the application logic will never flow into the shopping cart or check out processing.

To use these tools correctly, the testers and security team need to coordinate how and when the scans are set up to run. Testers often use a testing suite, like Selenium, to manage the testing process and record testing steps for later playback as the application changes or new features are added.

The DAST tool can use the Selenium test scripts to replay the testing, but instead of entering data appropriate for the entry field, the tool will use attack strings (like a XSS injection string) in as many different variations of them as it's programmed to test, then review the HTML page that's received back from the server to determine if the attack succeeded or not. SAST tools can load up several thousand test cases with different malicious payloads that are relevant to that application and are in-line with the recorded testing steps.

Black box testing helps to identify potential security vulnerabilities within commercial and proprietary Web applications when the source code is not available for review and analysis. If you implement a DAST solution from the same provider of SAST or SCA tools, you may be able to take advantage of an interface that's consistent for developers to use for processing reported defects, rather than needing to learn an entirely different tool. As much as possible, the processes and workflows you established to process the results from SAST tools should be reused for DAST, since adoption will be simpler than adding yet another security process to the heap.

Here are a few of the most popular black box penetration testing tools and suites:

- Vercode DAST[4]
- AppScan Enterprise (ASE)[5]
- Fortify WebInspect[6]

Although it's beyond the scope of this book to offer exhaustive coverage of DAST tools and how they work, a typical DAST product looks for and reports on the following vulnerabilities:

- Improper input validation
- Command injection and buffer overflow attacks
- SQL injection attacks
- Cross-site scripting vulnerabilities
- Cross-site request forgeries
- Directory traversal attacks
- Broken session management
- Broken or defective authorization and access control mechanisms

Since DAST looks at the application from an attacker point of view on a running version of the application, it can detect defects that SAST tools can't, providing you with valuable information about vulnerabilities that remain in the application that you can remediate before a malevolent outsider discovers them for you!

9.7 Deployment Strategies

Most often, people consider automated security testing tools as "too dangerous" in the hands of a malicious insider, organizations typically restrict their availability to only the security team or the Scrum tester role once they've been fully training and "checked-out" for use of the tool on organizational assets. Just as a car can be used for good or evil, black box testing tools can either help an organization with their software security or turn them into a victim of a malicious user intending as much harm possible in the shortest period of time possible without ever being caught.

Some of the commercial tools provide restricted Web-based access to developers (in Dev or QA environments only) in order to scan specific IP addresses where their applications under development are deployed. Such tools provide for restricted developer testing during development, while other configurations are used for centralized QA testing for governance and management of the software development life cycle.

9.7.1 Developer Testing

For Web applications when the application development architecture and development methodology permit, providing restricted access to a black box scanning tool to the developers of the application is usually recommended in the spirit of Shift Left, since security vulnerabilities discovered early in the life cycle prevent security defects from entering the integration or build testing phases, similar to the deployment of source code analyzers in the same environment. Repeated testing is often needed since the application changes with each release. Remember, DAST runs can take hours or days to complete.

9.7.2 Centralized Quality Assurance Testing

Apart from providing developers access to the black box tool, the quality assurance (QA) team or knowledgeable testers on a Scrum team should also have access to these tools. The testing carried out by this independent team might also serve as gating criteria for promoting the application QA testing and production environments. The results from these test results should be shared with the developers quickly after the tests are run, so they can develop strategies for fixing the problems that are uncovered. Once the criteria for moving to production are met, the QA team should sign off on the security vulnerability testing, along with the other test results (functional testing, user acceptance testing, etc.).

Centralized pen testing also ensures that other minor feature additions and bug fixes are also tested for security defects before they too are deployed to production.

9.8 Gray Box Testing

A combination of black box testing and white box testing, referred to as gray box testing, is the most widely used methodology by organizations that want a high level of assurance in their security testing processes. A team of security experts (on staff or contracted) is engaged to review the design and source code for an "inside-out" view of the application. A review and analysis of the application from a hacker's perspective provides the "outside-in" view of the application. The security team analyzes and correlates the results from both types of reviews and eliminates possible false positives. You need both types of reviews for assurance that a secure and resilient application development methodology is present and working as you intended.

9.9 Limitations and Constraints of Pen Testing

To expand on the point earlier, automated testing on an entire system requires that the testing tool be able to log in to the application just as an end user would to access the security-relevant parts of the program or system. An e-banking application provides a robust example. For any nontrivial features of the application (e.g., paying bills, checking balances, applying for loans or credit cards), a log-in is required so the application can properly identify the customer and only provide information related to that customer's accounts. Pen testing tools require the same access if they are being used to access the security of protected Web forms and functions. Most products allow you to configure the credentials needed, but it is vital that the test accounts that are used for logging in are reflective enough of real-life data. As a result, it's vital that the testing environment mirror the Production environment as much as possible, and since testing in production is a universal violation of best practices and most regulations, you have little choice but to assure that your QA test environment can behave nearly identically to your production environment, without the risks of using real-life data for testing purposes.

9.10 Interactive Application Security Testing (IAST)

An emerging technology, Interactive Application Security Testing (IAST)[7] tools help with identifying and managing security risks of software vulnerabilities discovered in running Web applications using dynamic testing (often referred to as runtime testing) techniques. IAST works through software instrumentation, or the use of instruments to monitor an application as it runs and gather information about what it does and how it performs. IAST tools work by instrumenting applications through agents and sensors in running applications and continuously analyze all application interactions initiated by manual tests, automated tests, or a combination of both to identify vulnerabilities in real time. In addition, some products integrate software composition analysis (SCA) tools to address known vulnerabilities in open source components and frameworks.

IAST automatically identifies and diagnoses software vulnerabilities in applications and Application Programming Interfaces (APIs). Jeff Williams, the CEO of Contrast Security and one of the founding members of OWASP says,[8] "IAST's better name might be '*Instrumented* Application Security Testing.' IAST is not a scanner. It continuously monitors your applications for vulnerabilities from within. IAST runs throughout your development lifecycle and instantly alerts you through the tools you're already using in development and test."

The key distinguishing feature of IAST is that it uses instrumentation to gather security information and telemetry directly from running code, rather than scanning source code (SAST) or HTTP scanning (DAST). You can start using IAST in your IDE as soon as you write and test your first lines of code.

Some of the popular IAST tools are available from:

- Contrast Security Assess[9]
- WhiteHat Security IAST[10]
- Checkmarx IAST[11]

9.11 Runtime Application Self-Protection (RASP)

RASP is another contribution to the alphabet soup of appsec tools. According to a TechBeacon article,[12] "RASP is a technology that runs on a server and kicks in when an application runs. It's designed to detect attacks on an application in real time. When an application begins to run, RASP can protect it from malicious input or behavior by analyzing both the app's behavior and the context of that behavior. By using the app to continuously monitor its own behavior, attacks can be identified and mitigated immediately without human intervention."

RASP builds security into a running application wherever it resides on a server, usually through agents. It intercepts all calls from the application to a system, making sure they're secure, and validates data requests directly inside the application. Both Web and non-Web apps may be protected by RASP. The technology doesn't affect the design of the application because RASP's detection and protection features run independently on the server the application hosts.

Some of the popular RASP technologies include:

- Signal Sciences RASP[13]
- Contrast Protect[14]
- Fortify Application Defender[15]
- Imperva RASP[16]

9.12 Summary

In Chapter 9 you saw various ways that professionals address software development and running software using testing and runtime tools for security and resilience. We looked at tools for manual and automated penetration testing, Dynamic Application Security Testing (DAST), Interactive Application Security Testing (IAST), and Runtime Application Self-Protection (RASP).

In Chapter 10, we'll take a deeper look into securing the DevOps environment and look at an ecosystem that brings together these tools and techniques into an orchestrated process that helps to assure security and resilience across every element of the SDLC.

References

1. Open Source Security Testing Methodology Manual (OSSTMM). (n.d.). Retrieved from http://www.isecom.org/research/osstmm.html
2. The Open Source Cybersecurity Playbook. (n.d.). Retrieved from http://www.ise com.org/research/playbook.html
3. Category:OWASP Application Security Verification Standard Project. (n.d.). Retrieved from https://www.owasp.org/index.php/Category:OWASP_ Application_Security_Verification_Standard_Project
4. DAST Product Page. (2019, February 21). Retrieved from https://www.veracode. com/products/dynamic-analysis-dast
5. IBM Knowledge Center. (n.d.). Retrieved from https://www.ibm.com/support/ knowledgecenter/en/SSW2NF_9.0.0/com.ibm.ase.help.doc/topics/c_intro_ase. html
6. Dynamic Application Security Testing (DAST): Web Dynamic Analysis Tool. (n.d.). Retrieved from https://www.microfocus.com/en-us/products/webinspect- dynamic-analysis-dast/overview
7. What is IAST? Interactive Application Security Testing. (2019, March 13). Retrieved from https://www.synopsys.com/software-integrity/resources/knowledge- database/what-is-iast.html
8. Introduction to IAST. (n.d.). Retrieved from https://dzone.com/refcardz/introduction- to-iast?chapter=1
9. Contrast Security (n.d.). Contrast Assess|Interactive Application Security Testing| IAST. Retrieved from https://www.contrastsecurity.com/interactive-application- security-testing-iast
10. Interactive Application Security Testing (IAST). (n.d.). Retrieved from https:// www.whitehatsec.com/products/dynamic-application-security-testing/interactive- application-security-testing/
11. An introduction to IAST. (2017, July 13). Retrieved from https://www.checkmarx. com/2017/07/13/an-introduction-to-iast/
12. Mello, J. P., Jr. (2016, March 17). What Is Runtime Application Self-Protection (RASP)? Retrieved from https://techbeacon.com/security/what-runtime-application- self-protection-rasp
13. Signal Sciences. (n.d.). RASP—Server Module. Retrieved from https://www.signal sciences.com/rasp-runtime-application-self-protection/
14. Contrast Security (n.d.). Contrast Protect|Runtime Application Self-Protection| RASP. Retrieved from https://www.contrastsecurity.com/runtime-application- self-protection-rasp
15. Runtime Application Self-Protection (RASP) Security Solutions. (n.d.). Retrieved from https://www.microfocus.com/en-us/products/application-defender/overview
16. RASP Market Leader | Secure all Applications by Default | Imperva. (n.d.). Retrieved from https://www.imperva.com/products/runtime-application-self- protection-rasp/

Chapter 10

Securing DevOps

In Chapters 4 through 9, we examined how agility can be used to transform the Scrum process into a secure software development lifecycle (SDLC) using strategies such as shift left and build security in. This transformation is extensible into the deployment and operations side of the software environment as well.

In Chapter 2, we introduced the concept of DevSecOps as an implementation of these principles and strategies. In Chapter 10, we'll dig deeper into DevSecOps and find ways to help apply these activities into your own secure SDLC and to measure the maturity of your practices.

10.1 Overview

Figure 10.1, introduced in Chapter 2, is what DevOps looks like when comprehensive security controls transform it into DevSecOps.[1]

10.2 Challenges When Moving to a DevOps World

Getting your SDLC to this point is rather challenging and requires foundational and fundamental changes in attitudes, culture, enhanced skills, and up-rooted old ways in how an organization conducts software development and operates the environment.

The Scrum process alone requires tremendous shifts in paradigms for everyone who touches how software is produced, and DevSecOps further extends the

DevSecOps cycle

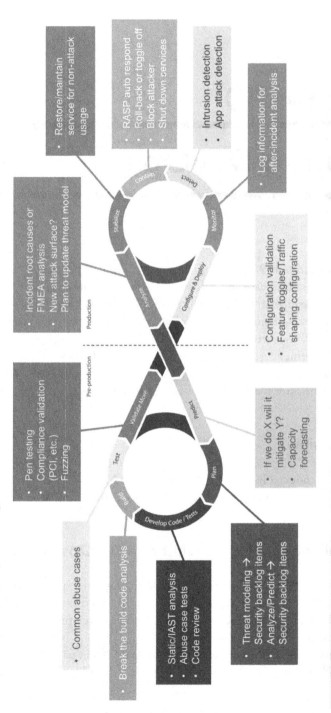

Figure 10.1 DevSecOps Cycle (*Source:* https://twitter.com/lmaccherone/status/843647960797888512. Used with permission of L. Maccherone, Jr.)

shifting paradigm and requires a culture change before any new environment can become effective—and secured!

10.2.1 Changing the Business Culture

Capgemini, a large IT consulting and services firm suggests:

> *"Digital organizations aspire to be agile like Amazon and Netflix, to innovate, to adapt, and to remain resilient against the cyber security challenges we face in today's digital world. Security needs to keep pace to enable an organization's accelerated IT delivery initiatives."*[2]

Capgemini states that transforming to DevSecOps is rooted in four guiding principles:

- **Educate.** Embed security into the design and cultivate a collaborative, "security-enabling business" mindset.
- **Automate.** Automate the SDLC pipeline and its security at every opportunity.
- **Monitor.** Take a risk-based approach to code review, application testing, and monitoring.
- **Iterate.** Strive for continuous security improvements through achievable iterations.

The SANS Institute offers an easy-to-remember mnemonic—CALMS—as guiding principles for building a DevSecOps Program.

- **Culture**
  - Break down barriers between development, security, and operations through education and outreach.
- **Automation**
  - Embed self-service automated security scanning and testing in continuous delivery.
- **Lean**
  - Value stream analysis on security and compliance processes to optimize flow.
- **Measurement**
  - Use metrics to shape design and drive decisions.
- **Sharing**
  - Share threats, risks, and vulnerabilities by adding them to engineering backlogs.

As you see, culture plays a vitally important role that needs addressing first. These cultural changes are required for any shift to DevOps. McKinsey, a global management consulting firm, identifies five key characteristics[3] that are required for a successful transformation to a DevOps culture:

1. **Push change from the top.** Start it from the bottom. Change, especially cultural change, doesn't happen without top-down sponsorship but won't take hold until it's executed at the smallest unit possible. Implementing DevOps at the team level, for example, enables the ability to demonstrate what is possible, locate obstacles, and break through them while the issues are still small enough to handle. Successful transformations are usually a continuous improvement journey rather than a *big bang* execution.

2. **Reimagine trust.** Traditionally, organizations establish trust through audit-based control frameworks designed to improve quality, assurance, security, compliance, and risk mitigation via checklists and audits of activity. DevOps doesn't work that way. It requires control functions to trust that product teams can and will be responsible stewards of organization-wide principles and requirements. Clearly trust needs to be earned, but this usually happens quickly when teams collaborate and demonstrate success through small pilots before scaling initiatives. This trust leads to empowering product teams to execute changes that are right and safe for the organization.

3. **Design for autonomy and empowerment.** DevOps requires engineering teams to *own control responsibilities* formerly owned by other functions. Engineering teams empowered to push change through to production must embed controls (automate) in their processes to give the organization confidence that testing, risk management, and escalation protocols are in place. Control must be designed into the process right from the start. It's about reimagining how controls are implemented to ensure they *happen by default* within the process without the external interference that usually causes bottlenecks.

4. **Crave improvement through testing.** The hunger to improve—the process, the quality, the speed, the impact of every single person—must pervade every corner of the organization. That requires changing mind-sets from *"Let's make it perfect"* to *"Good enough, let's see how it works and continue to iterate."* Supporting this cultural change requires putting in place flexible systems and ways of working to identify issues and opportunities, rapidly make adjustments, and test again.

5. **Measure and reward the result, not process compliance.** Cultures change when people are measured and rewarded for the right things. Everything, from performance contracts at the C-level to weekly

objectives for sysadmins, needs to be aligned with strategic business outcomes and the behaviors required to achieve them.

Culture changes in organizations take time and effort, but early results are possible as shifting paradigms produce positive visible results, and others begin to hop on board to take part in the transformation and gain their own positive results. In other words, small successes breed larger successes over time.

10.3 The Three Ways That Make DevOps Work

In the de-facto Bible for DevOps, *The DevOps Handbook*,[4] Kim et al. note that all DevOps patterns are derived from The Three Ways[5] to frame processes, procedures, practices, and prescriptive advice. The Three Ways are shown in Figures 10.2 through 10.4.

The First Way emphasizes the performance of the entire system, as opposed to the performance of a specific silo of work or department; this as can be as large a division (e.g., development or IT operations) or as small as an individual contributor (e.g., a developer, a system administrator). The focus is on all business value streams that are enabled by IT. In other words, it begins when requirements are identified (e.g., by the business or IT), are built in Development, and then transitioned into IT Operations, where the value is then delivered to the customer as a form of a service. Outcomes of putting The First Way into practice include never passing a known defect to downstream

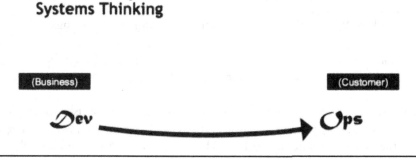

Figure 10.2 The Three Ways for DevOps—The First Way: Systems Thinking. (*Source*: Kim, G., Humble, J., Debois, P., and Willis, J. [2016]. *The DevOps Handbook: How to Create World-Class Agility, Reliability, and Security in Technology Organizations*. IT Revolution Press.[6] Used with permission.)

work centers, never allowing local optimization to create global degradation, always seeking to increase flow, and always seeking to achieve profound understanding of the system.

The Second Way is about creating the right-to-left feedback loops. The goal of almost any process improvement initiative is to *shorten and amplify feedback loops* so necessary corrections can be continually made. Outcomes of The Second Way include understanding and responding to all customers, internal and external; shortening and amplifying all feedback loops; and embedding knowledge where we need it.

The Second Way:
Amplify Feedback Loops

Figure 10.3 The Three Ways for DevOps—The Second Way: Amplify Feedback Loops (*Source*: Kim, G., Humble, J., Debois, P., and Willis, J. [2016]. *The DevOps Handbook: How to Create World-Class Agility, Reliability, and Security in Technology Organizations*. IT Revolution Press.[6] Used with permission.)

The Third Way is about creating a culture that fosters two things:

- Continual experimentation, taking risks, and learning from failure
- Understanding that repetition and practice is the prerequisite to mastery

Both of these are needed equally. Experimentation and taking risks ensure that people will regularly push to improve, even if it means going deeper into danger zones they've never gone into before. Mastery of these skills can also help to retreat out of a danger zone when you've gone too far. The outcomes of The Third Way include allocating time for the *improvement of daily work, creating rituals that reward the team for taking risks, and introducing faults into the system to increase resilience.*

The Third Way:
Culture Of Continual Experimentation And
Learning

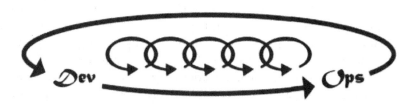

Figure 10.4   The Three Ways for DevOps—The Third Way: Culture of Continual Experimentation and Learning (*Source*: Kim, G., Humble, J., Debois, P., and Willis, J. [2016]. *The DevOps Handbook: How to Create World-Class Agility, Reliability, and Security in Technology Organizations*. IT Revolution Press.[6] Used with permission.)

An important lesson for those on security teams comes from *The DevOps Handbook*[6]:

> *"One of the top objections to implementing DevOps principles and patterns has been, 'Information security and compliance won't let us.' And yet, DevOps may be one of the best ways to better integrate information security into the daily work of everyone in the technology value stream."*

10.4 The Three Ways Applied to AppSec

In a Synopsys® Whitepaper entitled, "How to Navigate the Intersection of DevOps and Security,"[7] the writers suggest the following to help transform DevOps into DevSecOps:

- Integrating security into defect tracking and postmortems
  - Track security issues in the same work-tracking systems that your development and operations teams already use to ensure security visibility and prioritization. The most common tool is Jira®, Atlassian®'s issue and project tracking software. Then do a review after every security issue so you can prevent your team from repeating the same problems.
- Integrating security controls into shared source code repositories and services

- All teams should share a source code repository containing security-approved libraries that fulfill specific security objectives. This repository can also contain packages and builds approved for use in development (such as secure versions of OpenSSL with correct configurations), as well as toolchains, the deployment pipeline, and standards.
- Integrating security into your deployment pipeline
  - Automate as many security tests as possible, when possible, to run alongside other automated tests in your deployment pipeline. Automate these tests at every major commit of code by development or operations, even at very early stages. The goal is to provide short feedback loops, so development and operations teams are notified of any potential security issues in code commits. This allows teams to detect and correct security problems quickly as a part of daily work instead of waiting until the end of the SDLC, when fixes are often complex, time-consuming, and expensive.
- Ensuring the security of the application
  - As you automate your tests, generate tests to run continuously in your deployment pipeline, instead of performing unit or functional tests manually. This step is critical for the QA team, which will want to include static and dynamic analysis tests (SAST and DAST), software composition analysis (SCA), interactive application security tests (IAST), and more. Many of these testing processes can be part of a continuous integration (CI) or continuous delivery/deployment (CD) pipeline.
- Ensuring the security of the software supply chain
  - Up to 90% of modern applications are constructed from open source components, making them a fundamental part of the software supply chain today. When using open source components and libraries, DevOps teams must consider that applications inherit both the functionality of open source code and any security vulnerabilities it contains. Detecting known vulnerabilities in open source helps developers choose which components and versions to use. Integrating vulnerability checking during the CI process or within the binary repository or IDE helps ensure the security of the software supply chain.

The SANS Institute published a Secure DevOps Toolchain poster[8] to help appsec professionals select and evaluate potential tools for use in their own environments. Every implementation of Agile and DevSecOps is unique in many ways, so there is no single environment that addresses every need for everyone. There are dozens of Open Source projects that provide free resources to help you with your efforts. The poster details the sets of open source tools that apply to these activities:

- Pre-commit
  - Activities before code is checked in to version control
- Commit (continuous integration)
  - Fast, automated security checks during build and continuous integration steps
- Acceptance (continuous delivery)
  - Automated security acceptance, functional testing, and deep out-of-band scanning during continuous delivery
- Production (continuous deployment)
  - Security checks before, during, and after code is deployed to production
- Operations
  - Continuous security monitoring, testing, audit, and compliance checking

Establishing, using, and maintaining a DevSecOps environment can yield the kinds of efficiencies and improvements you expect, but these efforts won't come easily, quickly, or correctly the first few times through. As you gain experience and collect data, you can rapidly adjust to reduce problems you encounter and add additional controls to move into higher areas of maturity.

To help with measuring that progress, we turn to a DevSecOps Maturity Model from OWASP.

10.5 OWASP's DevSecOps Maturity Model

Attackers are intelligent and creative and are equipped with new technologies and purpose. Using the guidance of the forward-looking DevSecOps Maturity Model,[9] appropriate principles and measures are offered to help with countering the attacks, measure today's state of the program, and help with future plans.

The model contains 16 Dimensions[10] of DevSecOps that are measured across four levels. The 16 dimensions include:

- Build
- Deployment
- Education and guidance
- Culture and org
- Process
- Monitoring
- Logging
- Infrastructure hardening
- Patch management

- Dynamic depth for application
- Static depth for applications
- Test-intensity
- Consolidation
- Application tests
- Dynamic depth for infrastructure
- Static depth for infrastructure

The four maturity levels are:

- Level 1: Basic understanding of security practices
- Level 2: Understanding of security practices
- Level 3: High understanding of security practices
- Level 4: Advanced understanding of security practices at scale

For each dimension under each maturity level, you'll find a link that describes the risk and opportunity for that dimension, along with related details of exploitation to help you determine where your practices for that dimension appear. The model is also useful in understanding the dimensions of the next level of maturity to help you plan your program's future activities.

10.6 OWASP's DevSecOps Studio

DevSecOps Studio[11] is a virtual environment to learn and teach DevSecOps concepts.

The project is a free and open software to help more people learn about DevSecOps. The studio aims to help you to set up a reproducible DevSecOps Lab environment for learning and testing different tools in an experimental environment.

DevSecOps Studio[12]:

- Makes it easy to set up the environment for training/demos
- Is mostly automatic
- Teaches Security as Code, Compliance as Code, and Infrastructure as Code
- Has built-in support for CI/CD pipeline
- Security tools can be added as jobs to DevSecOps Studio.

10.7 Summary

In Chapter 10, we explored the roots of DevOps and The Three Ways that describe any of the DevOps implementation techniques. We then looked at the complexity of enriching DevOps with controls, tools, and processes to transform it into DevSecOps, where in-control pipelines for software development and deployment are hardened to help assure security and resilience along every process that touches custom-developed software. Finally, we learned about the OWASP DevSecOps Maturity Model and how it's applied and the OWASP DevSecOps Studio, with which you can put your ideas to the test before you commit to durable changes.

References

1. Maccherone, L. (2017, March 19). *DevSecOps Cycle* [Diagram]. Retrieved from https://twitter.com/lmaccherone/status/843647960797888512

2. Capgemini. (2019, June 12). DevSecOps—Security in Fast Digital. Retrieved from https://www.capgemini.com/gb-en/service/cybersecurity-services/devsecops-security-in-fast-digital/

3. Das, L., Lau, L., and Smith, C. (2017, February 26). Five Cultural Changes You Need for DevOps to Work. Retrieved from https://www.mckinsey.com/business-functions/digital-mckinsey/our-insights/digital-blog/five-cultural-changes-you-need-for-devops-to-work

4. Kim, G., Humble, J., Debois, P., and Willis, J. (2016). *The DevOps Handbook: How to Create World-Class Agility, Reliability, and Security in Technology Organizations*. IT Revolution Press

5. Kim, G. (2012, August 22). The Three Ways: The Principles Underpinning DevOps. Retrieved from https://itrevolution.com/the-three-ways-principles-underpinning-devops/

6. Kim, G., Humble, J., Debois, P., & Willis, J. (2016). *The DevOps Handbook: How to Create World-Class Agility, Reliability, and Security in Technology Organizations*. IT Revolution Press.

7. Synopsis®. (2019, May 23). DevSecOps: The Intersection of DevOps & Security. Retrieved from https://www.synopsys.com/software-integrity/solutions/by-security-need/devsecops.html

8. SANS Institute. (n.d.). Secure DevOps Tool Chain. Retrieved from https://www.sans.org/security-resources/posters/appsec/secure-devops-toolchain-swat-checklist-60

9. OWASP. (n.d.). DevSecOps Maturity Model. Retrieved from https://www.owasp.org/index.php/OWASP_DevSecOps_Maturity_Model

10. OWASP. (n.d.). DevSecOps Activities Overview. Retrieved from https://dsomm.timo-pagel.de/

11. OWASP. (n.d.). DevSecOps Studio Project. Retrieved from https://www.owasp.org/index.php/OWASP_DevSecOps_Studio_Project

12. OWASP. (n.d.). DevSecOps Studio. Retrieved from https://2018.open-security-summit.org/outcomes/tracks/devsecops/working-sessions/owasp-devsecops-studio/

Chapter 11

Metrics and Models for AppSec Maturity

All roads lead to Rome. It makes no difference what path you take—as long as you continue to strive for improvement, your efforts will be rewarded. Although any methodology to get there will do, you have undoubtedly noticed by now that metrics and measurement are vital to assure that you are headed in the right direction for secure and resilient systems and software.

11.1 Chapter Overview

In Chapter 11, you will find a detailed examination of two measurement and metrics models intended to help you determine the baseline maturity of the secure development integration into your software development life cycle (SDLC) and determine the pathways to further improve the maturity of your program.

We'll take a look at the two leading software security maturity approaches:

- OWASP's Open Software Assurance Maturity Model (OpenSAMM)
- Building Security in Maturity Model (BSIMM v9)

11.2 Maturity Models for Security and Resilience

Jeremy Epstein, a senior computer scientist at SRI International, wrote about the value of a software security maturity model[1]:

> *"So how do security maturity models like OpenSAMM and BSIMM fit into this picture? Both have done a great job cataloging, updating, and organizing many of the 'rules of thumb' that have been used over the past few decades for investing in software assurance. By defining a common language to describe the techniques we use, these models will enable us to compare one organization to another and will help organizations understand areas where they may be more or less advanced than their peers. . . . Since these are process standards, not technical standards, moving in the direction of either BSIMM or OpenSAMM will help an organization advance—and waiting for the dust to settle just means it will take longer to catch up with other organizations. . . . [I]n short: do not let the perfect be the enemy of the good. For software assurance, it's time to get moving now."*

11.3 Software Assurance Maturity Model—OpenSAMM

OpenSAMM is an open framework developed by the Open Web Application Security Project (OWASP) to help organizations formulate and implement a strategy for software security that is tailored to the specific risks facing the organization. OpenSAMM offers a roadmap and a well-defined maturity model for secure software development and deployment, along with useful tools for self-assessment and planning. OpenSAMM comes as a 96-page PDF file with detailed descriptions of each core activity and corresponding security processes.[2]

The resources provided by OpenSAMM aid in:

- Evaluating an organization's existing software security practices
- Building a balanced software security program in well-defined iterations
- Demonstrating concrete improvements to a security assurance program
- Defining and measuring security-related activities within an organization

SAMM was defined with flexibility in mind so that it can be utilized by small, medium, and large organizations using any style of SDLC. The model can be applied organization-wide, for a single line of business, or even on an individual project.

OpenSAMM was beta released under a Creative Commons Attribution Share-Alike license. The original work was donated to OWASP and is currently being run as an OWASP project.

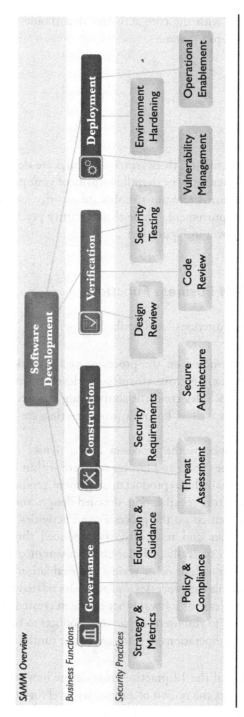

Figure 11.1 OpenSAMM Model (*Source: OpenSAMM by OWASP is licensed under CC-BY-SA*)

(See text describing Figure 11.1 on the following page.)

OpenSAMM starts with the core activities that should be present in any organization that develops software:

- Governance
- Construction
- Verification
- Deployment

In each of these core activities, three *security practices* are defined for 12 practices that are used to determine the overall maturity of your program. The security practices cover all areas relevant to software security assurance, and each provides a "silo" for improvement. These three security practices for each level of core activities are shown in Figure 11.1.

11.3.1 OpenSAMM Business Functions

Each of these business functions are described below:

- **Governance** is centered on the processes and activities related to how an organization manages overall software development activities. More specifically, this includes concerns confronting cross-cut groups involved in development as well as business processes that are established at the organization level.
- **Construction** concerns the processes and activities related to how an organization defines goals and creates software within development projects. In general, this includes product management, requirements gathering, high-level architecture specification, detailed design, and implementation.
- **Verification** is focused on the processes and activities related to how an organization checks and tests artifacts produced throughout software development. This typically includes quality assurance work such as testing, but it can also include other review and evaluation activities.
- **Deployment** entails the processes and activities related to how an organization manages release of software that has been created. This can involve shipping products to end users, deploying products to internal or external hosts, and normal operations of software in the runtime environment.

Objectives under each of the 12 practice areas define how it can be improved over time and establishes the notion of a maturity level for any given area. The three *maturity levels* for a practice correspond to:

(0: Implicit starting point with the practice unfulfilled)
1: Initial understanding and ad hoc provision of the practice
2: Increase efficiency and/or effectiveness of the practice
3: Comprehensive mastery of the practice at scale

11.3.2 Core Practice Areas

In this section we'll break down each of the practice areas into specific practices within it.

Governance Core Practice Areas

- **Strategy and Metrics (SM)** involves the overall strategic direction of the software assurance program and instrumentation of processes and activities to collect metrics about an organization's security posture.
- **Policy and Compliance (PC)** involves setting up a security and compliance control and audit framework throughout an organization to achieve increased assurance in software under construction and in operation.
- **Education and Guidance (EG)** involves increasing security knowledge among personnel in software development through training and guidance on security topics relevant to individual job functions.

Construction Core Practice Areas

- **Threat Assessment (TA)** involves accurately identifying and characterizing potential attacks on an organization's software in order to better understand the risks and facilitate risk management.
- **Security Requirements (SR)** involve promoting the inclusion of security-related requirements during the software development process in order to specify correct functionality from inception.
- **Secure Architecture (SA)** involves bolstering the design process with activities to promote secure-by-default designs and control over technologies and frameworks on which software is built.

Verification Core Practice Areas

- **Design Review (DR)** involves inspection of the artifacts created from the design process to ensure provision of adequate security mechanisms and adherence to an organization's expectations for security.

- **Code Review (CR)** involves assessment of an organization's source code to aid vulnerability discovery and related mitigation activities as well as establish a baseline for secure coding expectations.
- **Security Testing (ST)** involves testing the organization's software in its runtime environment in order to both discover vulnerabilities and establish a minimum standard for software releases.

Deployment Core Practice Areas

- **Vulnerability Management (VM)** involves establishing consistent processes for managing internal and external vulnerability reports to limit exposure and gather data to enhance the security assurance program.
- **Environment Hardening (EH)** involves implementing controls for the operating environment surrounding an organization's software to bolster the security posture of applications that have been deployed.
- **Operational Enablement (OE)** involves identifying and capturing security-relevant information needed by an operator to properly configure, deploy, and run an organization's software.

11.4 Levels of Maturity

Each core practice area is further detailed with a defined level of maturity using the following structure:

- Objective
- Activities
- Results
- Success Metrics
- Costs
- Personnel
- Related Levels

11.4.1 Objective

The *objective* is a general statement that captures the assurance goal of attaining the associated level. As the levels increase for a given practice, the objectives characterize more sophisticated goals in terms of building assurance for software development and deployment.

11.4.2 Activities

The *activities* are core requisites for attaining the Level. Some are meant to be performed organization-wide, and some correspond to actions for individual project teams. In either case, the activities capture the core security function, and organizations are free to determine how they fulfill the activities.

11.4.3 Results

The *results* characterize capabilities and deliverables obtained by achieving the given level. In some cases these are specified concretely; in others, a more qualitative statement is made about increased capability.

11.4.4 Success Metrics

The *success metrics* specify example measurements that can be used to check whether an organization is performing at the given level. Data collection and management are left to the choice of each organization, but recommended data sources and thresholds are provided.

11.4.5 Costs

The *costs* are qualitative statements about the expenses incurred by an organization attaining the given level. Although specific values will vary for each organization, these are meant to provide an idea of the one-time and ongoing costs associated with operating at a particular level.

11.4.6 Personnel

These properties of a level indicate the estimated ongoing overhead in terms of human resources for operating at the given level.

- Developers—individuals performing detailed design and implementation of the software
- Architects—individuals performing high-level design work and large-scale system engineering

- Managers—individuals performing day-to-day management of development staff
- QA testers—individuals performing quality assurance testing and pre-release verification of software
- Security auditors—individuals with technical security knowledge related to software being produced
- Business owners—individuals performing key decision making on software and its business requirements
- Support operations—individuals performing customer support or direct technical operations support

11.4.7 Related Levels

The *related levels* are references to levels within other practices that have some potential overlaps, depending on the organization's structure and progress in building an assurance program. Functionally, these indicate synergies or optimizations in activity implementation if the related level is also a goal or already in place.

11.4.8 Assurance

Because the 12 Practices are each a maturity area, the successive objectives represent the "building blocks" for any assurance program. OpenSAMM is designed for use in improving an assurance program in phases by:

- Selecting security practices to improve in the next phase of the assurance program
- Achieving the next objective in each practice by performing the corresponding activities at the specified success metrics

11.5 Using OpenSAMM to Assess Maturity Levels

Each security practice also includes an assessment worksheet, with the answers indicating the current level of maturity for that practice. A sample assessment worksheet extract for the education and guidance (EG) activities is shown in Figure 11.2.

Based on the scores assigned to each security practice, an organization can create a scorecard to capture those values. Functionally, a scorecard can be the

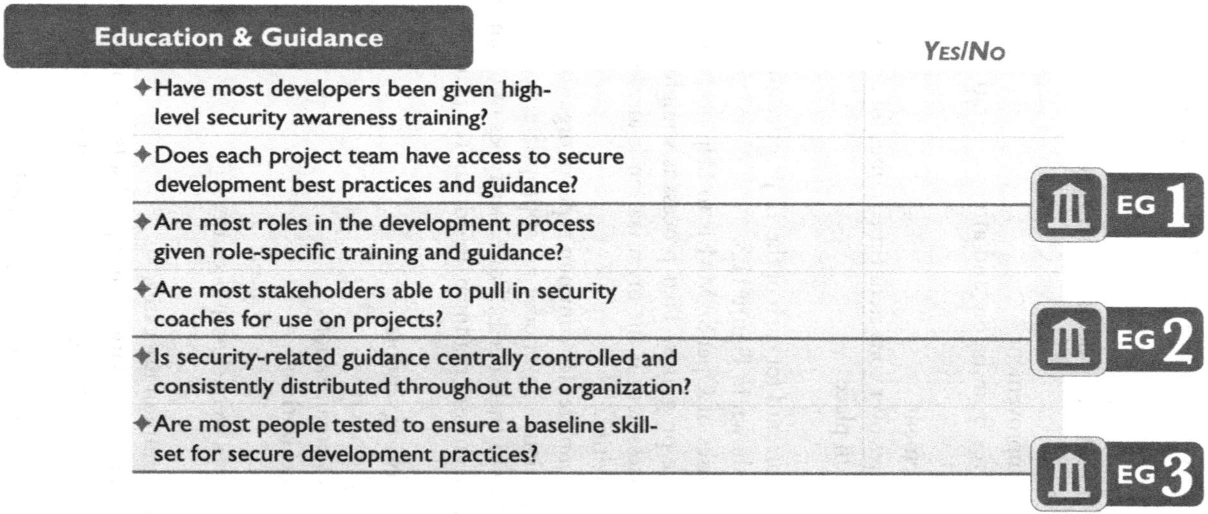

Education & Guidance

◆ Have most developers been given high-level security awareness training?

◆ Does each project team have access to secure development best practices and guidance?

◆ Are most roles in the development process given role-specific training and guidance?

◆ Are most stakeholders able to pull in security coaches for use on projects?

◆ Is security-related guidance centrally controlled and consistently distributed throughout the organization?

◆ Are most people tested to ensure a baseline skill-set for secure development practices?

Yᴇs/Nᴏ

EG 1

EG 2

EG 3

Figure 11.2 Sample OpenSAMM Assessment Worksheet Extract (*Source*: OpenSAMM by OWASP is licensed under CC-BY-SA)

simple set of 12 scores for a particular time. However, selecting a time interval over which to generate a scorecard facilitates understanding of overall changes in the assurance program during the time frame.

Using interval scorecards is encouraged for several situations:

- Gap analysis
  - Capturing scores from detailed assessments versus expected performance levels
- Demonstrating improvement
  - Capturing scores from before and after an iteration of assurance program build-out
- Ongoing measurement
  - Capturing scores over consistent time frames for an assurance program that is already in place

An example of a scorecard for each of the 12 practice areas with before-and-after measurements is shown in Figure 11.3.

One of the main uses of OpenSAMM is to help organizations build software security assurance programs. That process is straightforward and generally begins with an assessment if the organization is already performing some security assurance activities.

Several roadmap templates for common types of organizations are provided. Thus, many organizations can choose an appropriate match and then tailor the roadmap template to their needs. For other types of organizations, it may be necessary to build a custom roadmap. Roadmap templates are provided for:

- Independent software vendors
- Online service providers
- Financial services organizations
- Government organizations

These organization types were chosen because:

- They represent common use cases.
- Each organization has variations in typical software-induced risk.
- Optimal creation of an assurance program is different for each.

Roadmaps consist of phases in which several practices are each improved by one level. Building a roadmap entails selecting practices to improve in each planned phase. Organizations are free to plan into the future as far as they want, but they are encouraged to iterate based on business drivers and

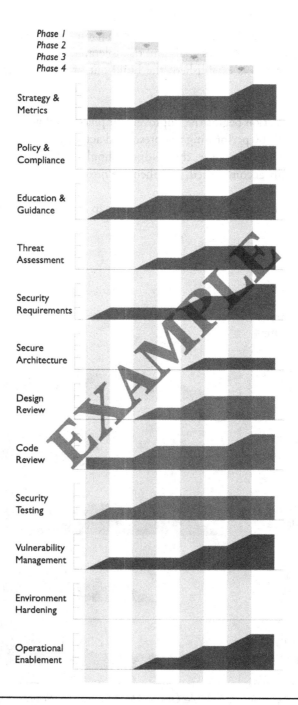

Phase 1
Phase 2
Phase 3
Phase 4

Strategy & Metrics

Policy & Compliance

Education & Guidance

Threat Assessment

Security Requirements

Secure Architecture

Design Review

Code Review

Security Testing

Vulnerability Management

Environment Hardening

Operational Enablement

Figure 11.3   Sample OpenSAMM Scorecard (*Source:* OpenSAMM by OWASP is licensed under CC-BY-SA)

organization-specific information to ensure that the assurance goals are commensurate with their business goals and risk tolerance.

Once a roadmap is established, the build-out of an assurance program is simplified.

- An organization begins the improvement phases and works to achieve the stated levels by performing the prescribed activities.
- At the end of each phase, the roadmap should be adjusted based on what was actually accomplished, and then the next phase can begin.

An extract of a sample OpenSAMM roadmap is shown in Figure 11.4.

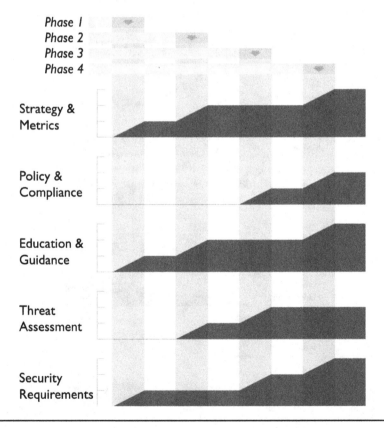

Figure 11.4 Excerpt of a Sample OpenSAMM Roadmap (*Source:* OpenSAMM by OWASP is licensed under CC-BY-SA)

11.6 The Building Security In Maturity Model (BSIMM)

The Building Security In Maturity Model (BSIMM)[3] is a study of existing software security initiatives. BSIMM is not a how-to guide, nor is it a one-size-fits-all prescription. The project's primary objective was to build a maturity model based on actual data gathered from nine large-scale software development initiatives. Representatives from Cigital® and Fortify® conducted interviews and collected data from nine original companies, including Adobe®, Dell® EMC®, Google™, Microsoft®, and five others. Using this data and conducting in-person executive interviews, the team developed a Software Security Framework (SSF) that creates buckets and three maturity levels for the 116 activities that they observed being performed in software development organizations. BSIMM has been updated over the course of its lifetime; now in its ninth edition, it includes new activities that have been added to clearly show that appsec in the cloud is becoming mainstream and indicates that activities observed among independent software vendors, Internet of Things (IoT) companies, and cloud firms have begun to converge, suggesting that common cloud architectures require similar software security approaches.

BSIMM is meant for use by anyone responsible for creating and executing a software security initiative (SSI). The authors of BSIMM observed that successful SSIs are typically run by a senior executive who reports to the highest levels in an organization. These executives lead an internal group that BSIMM refers to as the *software security group* (SSG), charged with directly executing or facilitating the activities described in the BSIMM. The BSIMM is written with the SSG and SSG leadership in mind.

11.7 BSIMM Organization

The model is divided into 12 practices, falling under four categories:

- Governance
- Intelligence
- Software security development lifecycle (SSDL) touchpoints
- Deployment

BSIMM indicates that SSGs should **emphasize security education and mentoring** rather than policing for security errors. BSIMM is not explicitly intended for software developers. Instead, it's intended for people who are *trying to teach software developers* how to do proper software security.

Properly used, BSIMM can help you determine where your organization stands with respect to real-world software security initiatives, what peers in your industry are doing, and what steps you can take to make your approach more effective.

A maturity model is appropriate because improving software security *almost always* means changing the way an organization works—something that never happens overnight. BSIMM provides a way to assess the state of an organization, prioritize changes, and demonstrate progress. Not all organizations need to reach the same security goals, but by applying BSIMM, all organizations can be *measured with the same yardstick.*

11.8 BSIMM Software Security Framework

The BSIMM Software Security Framework (SSF) is shown in Figure 11.5.

11.8.1 Governance

Governance includes those practices that help organize, manage, and measure a software security initiative. Staff development is also a central governance practice. In the governance domain, the strategy and metrics practice encompasses planning, assigning roles and responsibilities, identifying software security goals, determining budgets, and identifying metrics and gates. The compliance and policy practices focus on:

- Identifying controls for compliance requirements such as PCI-DSS and HIPAA
- Developing contractual controls such as service-level agreements to help control commercial off-the-shelf (COTS) software risk
- Setting organizational software security policy and auditing against that policy.
- Training, because it fills a critical role in software security—software developers and architects often start out with very little security knowledge.

11.8.2 Intelligence

Intelligence includes those practices that result in collections of corporate knowledge used in carrying out software security activities throughout the

Governance. Practices that help organize, manage, and measure a software security initiative. Staff development is also a central governance practice.

 Intelligence. Practices that result in collections of corporate knowledge used in carrying out software security activities throughout the organization. Collections include both proactive security guidance and organizational threat modeling.

 SSDL Touchpoints. Practices associated with analysis and assurance of particular software development artifacts and processes. All software security methodologies include these practices.

 Deployment. Practices that interface with traditional network security and software maintenance organizations. Software configuration, maintenance, and other environment issues have direct impact on software security.

Figure 11.5 The BSIMM Software Security Framework

organization. Collections include both proactive security guidance and organizational threat modeling.

The intelligence domain is meant to create organization-wide resources. Those resources are divided into three practices.

- Attack models capture information used to think like an attacker: threat modeling, abuse-case development and refinement, data classification, and technology-specific attack patterns.
- The security features and design practice are charged with creating usable security patterns for major security controls (meeting the standards defined in the next practice), building middleware frameworks for those controls, and creating and publishing other proactive security guidance.
- The standards and requirements practice involves eliciting explicit security requirements (nonfunctional requirements [NFRs] as acceptance criteria) from the organization, determining which COTS software to recommend, building standards for major security controls (such as authentication, input validation, etc.), creating security standards for technologies in use, and creating a standards review board.

11.8.3 SSDL Touchpoints

SSDL touchpoints include those practices associated with analysis and assurance of particular software development artifacts and processes. All software security methodologies include these practices.

The SSDL touchpoints domain is probably the most familiar of the four domains. This domain includes essential software security best practices that are integrated into the SDLC. The two most important software security practices are *architecture analysis* and *code review*.

Architecture analysis encompasses capturing software architecture in concise diagrams, applying lists of risks and threats, adopting a process for review (such as STRIDE or architectural risk analysis), and building an assessment and remediation plan for the organization.

The code review practice includes use of code review tools, development of customized rules, profiles for tool use by different roles (e.g., developers versus analysts), manual analysis, and tracking/measuring results. The security testing practice is concerned with prerelease testing, including integrating security into standard quality assurance processes. The practice includes use of black box security tools (including fuzz testing) as a smoke test in quality assurance, risk-driven white box testing, application of the attack model, and code coverage analysis. Security testing focuses on vulnerabilities in construction.

11.8.4 Deployment

Deployment includes those practices that interface with traditional network security and software maintenance organizations. Software configuration, maintenance, and other environment issues have direct impacts on software security.

By contrast, in the deployment domain, the penetration testing practice involves more standard outside-in testing of the sort carried out by security specialists. Penetration testing focuses on vulnerabilities in final configuration and provides direct feeds to defect management and mitigation. The software environment practice concerns itself with operating system and platform patching, web application firewalls, installation and configuration documentation, application monitoring, change management, and ultimately code signing. Finally, the configuration management and vulnerability management practice is concerned with patching and updating applications, version control, defect tracking and remediation, and incident handling.

11.9 BSIMM's 12 Practice Areas

Under each BSIMM category, there are a number of objectives and associated activities that determine the current level of maturity for that category. As you work your way down the list, the evidence of additional activities moves the organization further along the maturity levels, so that those organizations that claim to conduct all the activities in a specific category wind up as the most mature, at Level 3. The 12 practices are shown in Figure 11.6.

11.10 Measuring Results with BSIMM

Figure 11.7 shows a spider graph of the average maturity levels from the 120 organizations that have completed a BSIMM assessment by Synopsys®. The average maturity is used to compare a specific organization's maturity to help determine gaps and areas for improvement, as shown in the example in Figure 11.8.

11.11 The BSIMM Community

The 120 firms participating in BSIMM form the community. A private online community platform with nearly 600 members provides software security

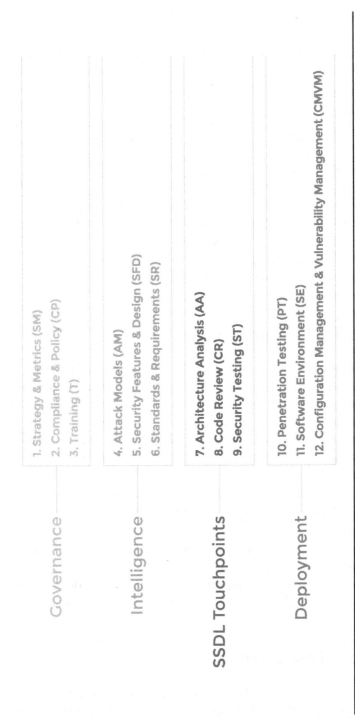

Governance
- 1. Strategy & Metrics (SM)
- 2. Compliance & Policy (CP)
- 3. Training (T)

Intelligence
- 4. Attack Models (AM)
- 5. Security Features & Design (SFD)
- 6. Standards & Requirements (SR)

SSDL Touchpoints
- 7. Architecture Analysis (AA)
- 8. Code Review (CR)
- 9. Security Testing (ST)

Deployment
- 10. Penetration Testing (PT)
- 11. Software Environment (SE)
- 12. Configuration Management & Vulnerability Management (CMVM)

Figure 11.6 BSIMM's 12 Practices (*Source*: BSIMM 9 by Gary McGraw, Ph.D., Sammy Migues, and Jacob West is licensed under CC-BY-SA)

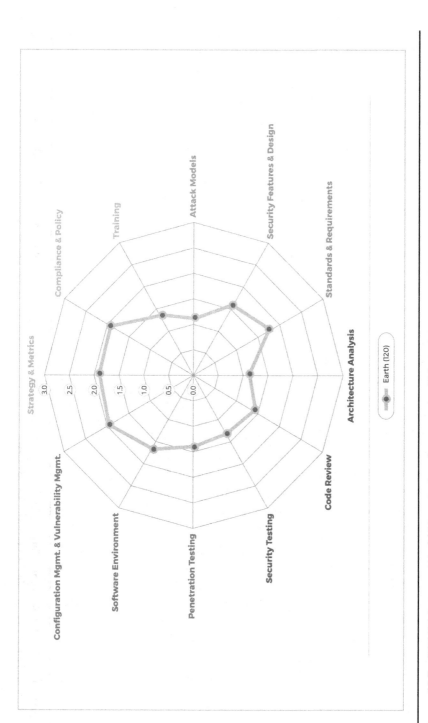

Figure 11.7 BSIMM Average World Maturity Levels across the 120 participants in BSIMM V9 (*Source:* BSIMM 9 by Gary McGraw, Ph.D., Sammy Migues, and Jacob West is licensed under CC-BY-SA)

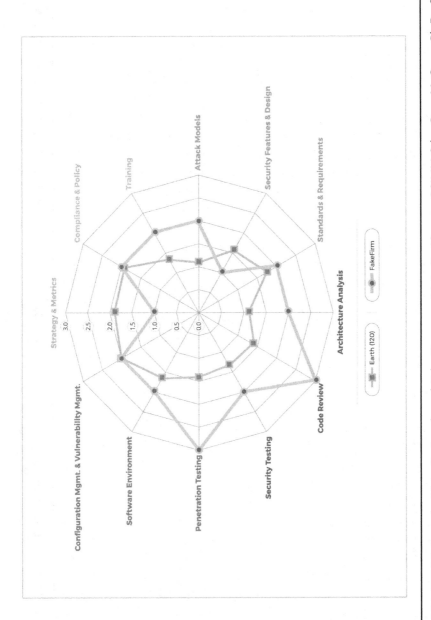

Figure 11.8 BSIMM Average Maturity Levels and Fake Company Maturity (*Source:* BSIMM 9 by Gary McGraw, Ph.D., Sammy Migues, and Jacob West is licensed under CC-BY-SA)

personnel a forum to discuss solutions with others who face the same issues, refine strategy with someone who has already addressed an issue, seek out mentors from those further along a career path, and band together to solve hard problems. Community members also receive exclusive access to topical webinars and other curated content. The BSIMM community also hosts annual private conferences during which representatives from each firm gather in an off-the-record forum to discuss software security initiatives.

11.12 Conducting a BSIMM Assessment

The BSIMM document is published under the Creative Commons Attribution-Share Alike 3.0 License, and you can use the documentation to conduct your own assessment for internal purposes. If you want your firm's data and outcomes included in the BSIMM Data Pool that's used for updating BSIMM, you'll need a contract with Synopsys to conduct an official assessment and report.

In preparation for that formal assessment, you'll need to consider which application development teams to engage for the interviews. BSIMM assessments are conducted as a series of interviews with SMEs and knowledgeable people in your organization who are involved with your SSI. You can slice the potential assessment population into any cross-sections that you'd like, but try to select those teams that represent actual outcomes from your efforts to roll out appsec. In other words, you want teams who have engaged in appsec practices you've helped to implement and are showing positive outcomes from those engagements. To gain a representative view of the SSI itself, you'll need a good cross-section of those whose lives you've touched with your program and who have a good understating of your mission and objectives for appsec.

11.13 Summary

In Chapter 11, you saw two approaches to developing, collecting, and assessing metrics to help determine an overall maturity level of your secure development implementation efforts and programs. Although both models should lead you to improved and measurable processes, selecting the one to use must be determined by your own organization's structure, its internal development processes, and your own good judgment. While we won't recommend one approach over the other, you should be able to see the overlaps between them and use the one that best fits your purposes. As we mentioned early in this chapter, don't let the perfect be the enemy of the good. For software assurance, the time to get moving is now!

References

1. Epstein, J. (n.d.) Jeremy Epstein on the Value of a Maturity Model. OpenSAMM. Retrieved from https://www.opensamm.org/2009/06/jeremy-epstein-on-the-value-of-a-maturity-model/
2. SAMM (n.d.). *Software Assurance Maturity Model (SAMM): A Guide to Building Security into Software Development.* Retrieved from http://www.opensamm.org/downloads/SAMM-1.0.pdf
3. BSIMM. (2019, July 19). About the Building Security In Maturity Model. Retrieved from https://www.bsimm.com/about.html

Chapter 12

Frontiers for AppSec

The stakes for software development teams (and the rest of us, actually) are already rather high and getting higher. On top of the countless changes in how software is developed, we have new and unexpected places where software showed up. The attack surface for software is growing exponentially as we see new technology and new ways of using software emerge and flourish.

Today, development teams are responsible not just for security, but for safety as well. Imagine trying to live with yourself knowing software you wrote was the cause of someone's death . . .

Those are the stakes and those most responsible for it need the right kinds of preparation.

In Chapter 12, we'll survey a potpourri of new technologies and new ways software is being packaged, deployed, and used across the world.

12.1 Internet of Things (IoT)

Here's just a fraction of IoT's reach in 2019:

- Wi-Fi-connected refrigerators, washers, and dryers
- Bluetooth-connected vaping devices
- Drones with cameras
- Voice-activated assistants
- Interactive toys
- Smart TVs

- Wearables
- Externally controlled implanted medical devices
- And let's not forget e-scooters roaming urban streets and sidewalks . . .

Someone is writing all the software for these *things,* but do they truly appreciate the awesome responsibility that goes along with it?

Because of IoT, software is forced into a state in which a *recall of a physical device* may be needed to remediate basic software defects or worse, security defects in the software. How will IoT firms respond? Who's willing to ship their refrigerator back for a software update?

12.1.1 The Industry Responds

The IoT Security Foundation is a non-profit organization that has been dedicated to driving security excellence since 2014. Their mission is a vendor-neutral, international initiative to serve as an expert resource for sharing knowledge, best practices, and advice. Their program is designed to propagate good security practice, increase adopter knowledge, and raise user confidence in IoT.[1]

The foundation publishes a series of best practice guides[2] on how to plan and develop IoT applications and devices with these goals in mind:

- Aid confident adoption of secure IoT solutions, enabling their technology benefits
- Influence the direction and scope of any future necessary regulation
- Influence IoT procurement requirements, including by governments
- Increase the levels of security expertise throughout the IoT sector
- Deliver business value to members by building an eminent, diverse, and international IoT security network

The Foundation's motto is:

Build Secure, Buy Secure, Be Secure

Their *Best Practice Guidelines* include:

- *Can You Trust Your Smart Building?*
- *IoT Security Reference Architecture for the Healthcare Industry*
- *IoT Security Compliance Framework*
- *IoT Security Compliance Questionnaire*
- *Secure Design Best Practice Guides*

- *Vulnerability Disclosure Best Practice Guide*
- *HOME IoT Security Architecture and Policy *FOR OEM's*
- *ENTERPRISE IoT Security Architecture and Policy *FOR SECURITY ARCHITECTS*
- *Establishing Principles for Internet of Things Security*
- *IoT Cybersecurity: Regulation Ready*
- *Understanding the Contemporary Use of Vulnerability Disclosure in Consumer IoT Products*

12.1.2 The Government Responds

In July 2019, the US National Institute of Standards and Technology (NIST) published a roadmap for IoT security: *The Core Cybersecurity Feature Baseline for Securable IoT Devices: A Starting Point for IoT Device Manufacturers* as NISTIR 8259.[3] The documents define a core baseline of cybersecurity features that manufacturers may voluntarily adopt for IoT devices they produce. It also provides information on how manufacturers can identify and implement features beyond the core baseline most appropriate for their customers. Draft NISTIR 8259 builds upon NIST's previous work, *Considerations for Managing Internet of Things (IoT) Cybersecurity and Privacy Risks.*[4] The roadmap covers:

- Cybersecurity Feature Identification
  - ○ Expected Customers and Use Cases
  - ○ Device Cybersecurity Features
- The Core Baseline for IoT Devices
- Cybersecurity Feature Implementation
  - ○ Device Specifications
  - ○ Cybersecurity Feature Inheritance
- Cybersecurity Information to Provide to Customers
- Secure Development Practices for IoT Devices

12.2 Blockchain

Blockchain, as a distributed ledger technology[5] that makes Bitcoin and hundreds of other cryptocurrencies possible, is touted as a tremendous advance in computer security. As people enter the mix, however, Blockchain often turns into a computer security liability.

Creative applications of Blockchain increase its appeal, but sometimes a system is turned against itself, as is the case with crypto-mining bot-controlled malware that steals computing resources for brute-force computations. We're all placed at risk when insecure user practices and defective application software allows for malware infections that may be impossible to remove. In addition, the private cryptographic keys that are needed to identify ownership or transaction outcomes are often the target of theft, which is only made easier when the software wallets to manage these keys are written with defective code.

12.2.1 Security Risks with Blockchain Implementations

In a *Practical Law* paper from Thomson-Reuters, entitled "Cybersecurity Tech Basics: Blockchain Technology Cyber Risks and Issues: Overview,"[6] the section on blockchain cyber vulnerabilities indicates three areas in which the creation and use of blockchains may be vulnerable to problems related to computer security.

- Blockchain code vulnerabilities
  - Blockchain applications are like any other computer system from the view that software coding errors can introduce cyber risks. Coding errors may be more likely to occur where network protocols implement unusual or novel functionality for which potential vulnerabilities are not yet well understood. For example, in 2016, hackers exploited a coding defect in the source code of the Decentralized Autonomous Organization (DAO), a virtual organization operated using smart contracts and built on the Ethereum® public blockchain, resulting in the theft of Ethereum tokens valued in excess of $50 million (at the time). Blockchain technology is also highly dependent on encryption algorithms. Commonly used encryption techniques are widely vetted and generally reliable. However, as computing techniques evolve, they may become more vulnerable to attack.
- Blockchain platform vulnerabilities
  - Blockchain applications typically run on general-purpose operating systems and platforms that are subject to known hardware and software vulnerabilities. Even special purpose blockchain platforms often depend on general-purpose hardware and software. Organizations must treat these environments like their other business-critical computing resources and follow generally accepted cybersecurity practices. Identifying and managing known vulnerabilities is a core element of any reasonable cybersecurity program.
- End-user vulnerabilities
  - The edge of any blockchain in which users interact with the system is often the gateway for cyberattacks. Cryptocurrency thefts typically

involve exploiting vulnerabilities in connected systems. Perhaps an online wallet is hacked, or a user's private key is stolen, allowing hackers to drain account balances. End-user vulnerabilities may allow attackers to infiltrate and compromise private blockchains by impersonating authorized users. Specific end-user vulnerabilities that organizations considering using blockchain applications should address include:

- **Private key management.** Blockchain network integrity depends on encryption algorithms, typically public–private key methods. Most reported blockchain-related cyberattacks have succeeded by stealing end users' keys, not by attacking the blockchain itself. Individuals may lose or misplace their private keys, resulting in the loss of blockchain-stored assets, because private keys are not reproducible by design. End users must understand and protect the private keys they hold on their systems or other media.

- **Wallet controls.** Service providers, such as digital wallet providers, have emerged to provide key management services and minimize individuals' risks. However, these services depend on passwords, device authentication (such as using a particular mobile phone), or other user authentication controls. Because they involve human interaction, these controls are vulnerable unless individuals and organizations take due care.

- **Impersonation, phishing, malware, and other end-user attacks.** Attackers can use general end-user attacks to gather user credentials or otherwise infiltrate blockchain applications. These attacks can be especially damaging to private blockchains that operate under less robust consensus mechanisms. Blockchain-stored assets remain at risk because private keys are not reproducible by design. End users must understand and protect the private keys they hold on their systems or other media.

12.2.2 Securing the Chain

Gemalto, an international provider of cryptographic-based systems, offers the following suggestions for securing the network for those working with developing and deploying blockchain technology[7]:

- Ensure strong identities and authentication
  - Provide strong identity and access controls to all devices and participants that use permissioned blockchains for which the identities of all participants are known. Devices should be identified using Public Key

Infrastructure technology for strong authentication and data encryption. Human users should be strongly authenticated to the network using multifactor authentication mechanisms to prevent credential compromises.

- Securing core blockchain technologies
  - Because public-key cryptography acts as the basic security foundation of any blockchain network, ensuring the safety of blockchain transactions by securely generating, using, and storing the crypto keys is of paramount importance. Further, because cryptography is used to sign smart contracts (to prove their origin) and secure the data stored both on and off the blockchain network to provide confidentiality of the transactions, securing the crypto keys becomes crucial.
- Securing blockchain communications
  - Secure generation and secure storage and use of all the cryptographic keys used in SSL and TLS network connections are needed as a secure method for exchanging messages and managing authentication to secure the integrity of all blockchain transactions.

Although blockchain may be one of the most secure data protection technologies available for use today, taking its security for granted is dangerous and risky. As the blockchain technology evolves, so will its vulnerabilities, and it's only a matter of time before hackers will find a way to breach blockchain networks. Organizations need to secure their blockchain right from the start (build security in by shifting left) through implementing strong authentication, employing cryptography key vaulting mechanisms, and of course implementing secure treatment of software within every step of the SDLC.

12.3 Microservices and APIs

As organizations began to migrate to new uses of cloud technology, such as Platform as a Service (PaaS), Infrastructure as a Service (IaaS), and containerization (discussed next), it became obvious that a *lift and shift* strategy was not going to fly. Rather, these new ways of operating data centers required rethinking how applications are built, deployed, and used. Large, monolithic applications started undergoing a refactoring process to break up the applications using some of the principles that we discussed in Chapters 5 and 6. This activity involves isolating functions (services) around a central concept or entity—for example, one microservice might deal with all the functions needed to create a client entity, another microservice might represent the sales entity, yet another might represent order processing, and so on. These microservices are activated using an application programming interface (API) that describes what functions are available to access and what attributes are involved. These APIs are most often developed using the Representational State Transition,[8] or REST, architectural style.

Application development using these microservices entails developing a series of API invocation processes that perform useful work without concern for how these services are implemented, while permitting enhancement and changes to occur without interface changes to isolate the need to rebuild every application that needs those services. This presents a challenge to application security testing. API code itself may be run through a scanner, but this likely won't find and report on vulnerabilities. As we saw in Chapter 8, an application needs data input sources and control flows for the scanner to detect vulnerabilities. An API—as code on its own—won't have those elements, and static code scanners might prove useless for API testing. Point solutions in the market may address these scanning needs but will run as developer-oriented tools that work inside the API development environment. It may prove challenging to establish a security policy on how these tools should be used and how they detect and risk-rate discovered defects.

The restfulapi.net website, established to collect, present, and distribute information deemed vital while building next-generation RESTful APIs, offers security design advice[9] for architects and designers:

- **Least privilege.** An entity should only have the required set of permissions to perform the actions for which they are authorized, and no more. Permissions can be added as needed and should be revoked when no longer in use.
- **Fail-safe defaults.** A user's default access level to any resource in the system should be "denied" unless they've been explicitly granted a "permit."
- **Economy of mechanism.** The design should be as simple as possible. All the component interfaces and the interactions between them should be simple enough to understand.
- **Complete mediation.** A system should validate access rights to all its resources to ensure that they're allowed and should not rely on a cached permission matrix. If the access level to a given resource is being revoked, but that isn't reflected in the permission matrix, it would violate the security.
- **Open design.** This principle highlights the importance of building a system in an open manner—with no secret, confidential algorithms.
- **Separation of privilege.** Granting permissions to an entity should not be purely based on a single condition; a combination of conditions based on the type of resource is a better idea.
- **Least common mechanism.** It concerns the risk of sharing state among different components. If one can corrupt the shared state, it can then corrupt all the other components that depend on it.

They also list these security best practices for both designers and developers:

- Keep it simple
- Use password hashes
- Never expose information on URLs
- Consider OAuth instead of basic authentication
- Add timestamps in request
- Input parameter validation
- Ensure psychological acceptability—security should not make the user experience worse

12.4 Containers

The next step beyond microservices and APIs is containerization of applications. A container[10] is a standard unit of software that packages code and dependencies so the application runs quickly and reliably from one computing environment to another. Docker is the present-day standard for creating container images. These images are lightweight, standalone, executable packages of software that include everything that's needed to run an application: code, runtime, system tools, system libraries, and settings. Containers isolate software from its environment and ensure that the applications work uniformly.

12.4.1 Container Security Issues

An article from *Container Journal*[11] outlines four areas of security that need attention:

- Container images
  - Container technology is dependent on images as the building blocks for containers. The technology enables developers to easily create their own images or download public files from sites like Docker Hub. However, images are not always easy to trust from a security perspective. The images must be signed and originate from a trusted registry to ensure high-quality protection. They also must get properly vetted and the code validated. If not, the images are vulnerable to cyberthreats.
- Kernel root accounts
  - Reducing the attack surface is a basic aspect of any security approach to help ensure that code with vulnerabilities does not enter into the environment. With containers, however, there are specialized structural

and operational elements that require extra attention. The configurations and container profiles must be maintained consistently to minimize security threats.

- User access control
  - Access controls need to be enforced for privileged accounts and operations accounts for the deployment pipeline. The approach helps with accountability and operational consistency related to effective access controls. It creates methods to pinpoint who made changes to container settings or configurations. It also helps discover who downloaded an image and if anyone started a container in production. However, it is important to note that although developers can get more access to what they need to get a job done, that does not always make it beneficial for security. Developers can get too much access to accounts, so applying centrally managed constraints on what changes or commands a user can make is essential.
- The web host
  - An attractive benefit of containers is that they can isolate an application and its dependencies within a self-contained unit that can run anywhere, but containerization poses some security vulnerabilities at the host level too. You need to be aware of how the container can impact the actual host and what measures are appropriate to ensure its safety. The authors recommended that safer-to-run container orchestration systems such as Kubernetes® in the cloud on Azure®, Google Cloud Platform (GCP), or Amazon Web Services® (AWS). Each has tools in place that can constrain what the unit can and cannot access. Traditional shared web hosting services often lack the same constraints, reducing securability of the processing.

12.4.2 NIST to the Rescue Again!

The NIST Special Publication 800-190, Application Container Security Guide (SP800-190),[12] explains the security concerns associated with container technologies and makes practical recommendations for addressing those concerns when planning for, implementing, and maintaining containers. SP800-190 offers recommendations in these areas to help appsec professionals address container risks before they manifest themselves:

- Countermeasures for major risks
  - Image countermeasures
    - Image vulnerabilities

- Image configuration defects
- Embedded malware
- Embedded clear text secrets
- Use of untrusted images
- Registry countermeasures
  - Insecure connections to registries
  - Stale images in registries
  - Insufficient authentication and authorization restrictions
- Orchestrator countermeasures
  - Unbounded administrative access
  - Unauthorized access
  - Poorly separated inter-container network traffic
  - Mixing of workload sensitivity levels
  - Orchestrator node trust
- Container countermeasures
  - Vulnerabilities within the runtime software
  - Unbounded network access from containers
  - Insecure container runtime configurations
  - App vulnerabilities
  - Rogue containers
- Host OS countermeasures
  - Large attack surface
  - Host OS component vulnerabilities
  - Host file system tampering
- Hardware countermeasures

12.5 Autonomous Vehicles

Although a book on application security for appsec professionals and software development teams and managers can barely scratch the surface of the security, societal, ethical, and legal issues related to autonomous vehicles, they're included here as a frontier for software professionals for completeness. Working on applications for self-driving vehicles requires exceptional personal responsibility to get it right the first time and know that you have.

Should you ever get involved in working on applications in the area of next-generation, self-driving cars, trucks, farm equipment, or whatever shape they take on in the future, you can refer to guidance developed to help people and manufacturers with the highest levels of security and safety. This time, guidance comes from the UK and British Standards Institute (BSI) in the form of *PAS 1885:2018—The Fundamental Principles of Automotive Cyber Security.*[13] (Also see *Introduction to Self-Driving Vehicle Technology.*[14])

The standard indicates that as vehicles get smarter and their connectivity and integration with outside systems increases, so too does the need for vehicle and vehicle–systems-related cyber security. PAS was written to help all parties involved in the vehicle lifecycle and ecosystem understand better how to improve and maintain vehicle security and the security of associated intelligent transport systems (ITS). For help in understanding the role and responsibilities of software development in the ecosystem of intelligent transport systems, PAS 1885:2018 is a good start to what will become a lengthy process for serious developers and stakeholders.

12.6 Web Application Firewalls (WAFs)

Web application firewalls (WAFs) are a control mechanism that operates in front of the web server load balancer. The WAF is programmed to recognize patterns of application attacks, such as Cross Site Scripting (XSS) and other injection attacks, and take some action before those are passed on the web application for processing. The actions they take are based on a policy the WAF is given to enforce. This policy can simply be to alert and report the possible attack, or it can block the traffic and prevent the exploit from succeeding. Because WAFs operate outside the knowledge of or involvement by the web application, the solution acts as a double-edged sword.

Developers may use its presence as an excuse for not paying sufficient attention to code-level defects they introduce or as a crutch, believing that the WAF will take care of their application's security. Both situations work against your efforts to secure the SDLC.

As an element in Defense in Depth, WAFs can be an excellent control to help prevent exploits, but it should not get in the way of efforts to drive human behavior that leads to defensive programming. One way to help prevent this from being a problem is using a WAF in enforcement mode **only** in production segments and not allowing the WAF to block the work of pen testers in QA as they try to find defects in applications; it does you no good that a WAF may *prevent proving* that a defect reported by a scanning tool exists. Testing the effectiveness of the WAF in the QA Environment **after** your application security testing steps are complete is one possible way to incorporate its use as an effective layer of defense.

12.7 Machine Learning/Artificial Intelligence

AI and machine learning especially, like self-driving vehicles, will keep computer scientists and security researchers busy for the foreseeable future. And like self-driving vehicles, we can barely scratch the surface here, but because AI and machine learning software, tools, and platforms (e.g., GCP®) are mostly free for the taking, more and more developers and interested IT professionals will engage with them sooner or later.

In his article entitled, "Security Problems of Machine Learning Models,"[15] author David Balaban points out:

> *"By machine learning, we usually understand such algorithms and mathematical models that are capable of learning and acting without human intervention and progressively improve their performance. In computer security, various machine learning methods have long been used in spam filtering, traffic analysis, fraud prevention, and malware detection. In a sense, this is a game where, by making a move, you expect the reaction of the enemy. Therefore, while playing this game, one has to constantly update and correct models, feeding them with new data, or even changing them completely. . . . As a result, future preference will be given to tools that use more intelligent techniques, such as machine learning methods. These allow you to identify new features automatically, can quickly process large amounts of information, generalize, and make quick and correct decisions. It is important to note that on the one hand, machine learning can be used for protection and on the other hand, it can also be used for more intelligent attacks."*

The article classifies attacks on machine learning models:

- By influence type
  - Causative attacks affect the learning of the model through interference with the training data sample.
  - Exploratory attacks use classifier vulnerabilities without affecting the training data set.
- By security violation
  - Integrity attacks compromise the system through type II (false negative) errors.
  - Availability attacks cause the system to be shut down, usually based on type I and type II errors.
- By specificity
  - A targeted attack is aimed at changing the prediction of the classifier when working with a particular class.
  - An indiscriminate attack is aimed at changing the response/decision of the classifier to any class, except the correct one.

In preventing or reducing the chance of attacks, the article offers this advice:

- If it is possible not to use machine learning models in a sensitive environment, it is better not to use them, at least until better protection methods appear.
- If the system is associated with performing important functions—for example, diagnosing diseases, detecting attacks on industrial facilities, or driving an unmanned vehicle—the consequences of compromising the security of such a system can be catastrophic.
- The problem of misclassifying malicious data samples is huge. If a model does not see such samples of malicious data in its training data set, the outcomes will be wrong. Try to supplement your training data set with all possible (and currently available) malicious data samples and prevent yourself from being deceived, at least by them.

12.8 Big Data

Technopedia describes[16] big data as a process that is used when traditional data mining and handling techniques cannot uncover the insights and meaning of the underlying data. Data that is unstructured, time sensitive, or simply very large cannot be processed by relational database engines. This type of data requires a different processing approach called *big data*, which uses massive parallelism on readily available hardware. Problems with security pose serious threats to any system. ScienceSoft, a US-based provider of IT and big data consulting services, reports[17] from their experts about the more insidious security challenges related to big data:

1. Vulnerability to fake data generation
2. Potential presence of untrusted mappers
3. Troubles of cryptographic protection
4. Possibility of sensitive information mining
5. Struggles of granular access control
6. Data provenance difficulties
7. High speed of NoSQL databases' evolution and lack of security focus
8. Absent security audits

12.8.1 Vulnerability to Fake Data Generation

To deliberately undermine the quality of your big data analysis, cybercriminals can fabricate data and "pour" it into your data lake. For instance, if your manufacturing company uses sensor data to detect malfunctioning production processes, cybercriminals can penetrate your system and make your sensors show fake results—say, wrong temperatures. This way, you can fail to notice alarming trends and miss the opportunity to solve problems before serious damage is caused. Such challenges can be solved through applying fraud detection approach.

12.8.2 Potential Presence of Untrusted Mappers

As big data is collected, it undergoes parallel processing. One of the methods used here is the MapReduce (MapR) paradigm. When the data is split into numerous bulks, a mapper processes them and allocates to particular storage options. If outsiders have access to your mapper's code, they can change the settings of the existing mappers or add "alien" ones. This way, your data processing can be effectively ruined: cybercriminals can make mappers produce inadequate lists of key/value pairs, leading to faulty results brought up by the Reduce process. Gaining such access may not be too difficult, because big data technologies generally don't provide an additional security layer to protect data and tend to rely on perimeter security systems.

12.8.3 Lack of Cryptographic Protection

Despite the opportunity to—and the need to—encrypt big data, cryptography is often ignored. Sensitive data is generally stored in the cloud without any encrypted protection. Although cryptographic countermeasures may slow down big data processing, negating its speed, data protection must remain paramount, especially when working with large datasets.

12.8.4 Possibility of Sensitive Information Mining

Related to lacking cryptography to prevent unauthorized access to sensitive data, other lacking or weak security controls may permit corrupt insider IT specialists or evil business rivals mine unprotected data and sell it for their own benefit. Here, data can be better protected by adding appropriate security and data access controls.

12.8.5 Problems with Granularity of Access Controls

Sometimes, data items fall under tight restrictions, and very few people have the authorization to view the data, such as personal information in medical records (name, email, blood sugar, etc.). But some unrestricted data elements could theoretically be helpful for users with no access to the secret data, such as medical researchers. With finer-grained access controls, people can access needed and authorized data sets but can view only the elements (attributes) they are allowed to see. Such access is difficult to grant and control, simply because big data technologies aren't initially designed to do so. One solution is to copy permissible datasets and data elements to a separate big data warehouse and provide access to a particular user as a group. For a medical research, for instance, only the medical info (without the names, addresses, and so on) would be copied.

12.8.6 Data Provenance Difficulties

Data provenance—or historical records about your data—complicates matters even more. Data provenance is a broad big-data concern, but from a security perspective, it is crucial because:

- Unauthorized changes in metadata can lead you to the wrong data sets, which will make it difficult to find needed information.
- Untraceable data sources can be a huge impediment to finding the roots of security breaches and fake data generation cases.

12.8.7 High Speed of NoSQL Databases' Evolution and Lack of Security Focus

The popularity of NoSQL databases (such as MongoDB) is huge when working in big data science, but security is often the last thing considered—if it's considered at all. These databases were never built with security in mind, so attempts to bolt it on are likely to lead to loss of access or loss of data.

12.8.8 Absent Security Audits

Big data security audits help companies gain awareness of their security gaps, though very few companies bother with them. There are several reasons that those who work with big data claim auditing is unnecessary: lack of time, resources, qualified personnel, or clarity of business-related security requirements.

12.9 Summary

In Chapter 12 we took a 10,000-foot fly over of trends and new uses for software that we could have never anticipated even a decade ago. These trends and new uses are raising the stakes for everyone across society as our world becomes more and more connected and automated. Although we could not possibly have covered all the changes happening in the IT world, you should now have a good sense of the areas of focus for today and tomorrow. Software professionals are undergoing a renaissance period in which art, science, technology, human ethics, and the choices developers make are shaping the future.

Let's all do our part to make it a promising one!

References

1. IoT Security Foundation. (n.d.). Our Mission. Retrieved from https://www.iotsecurityfoundation.org/about-us/
2. IoT Security Foundation. (n.d.). *Best Practice Guidelines*. Retrieved from https://www.iotsecurityfoundation.org/best-practice-guidelines/
3. NISTIR 8259 (DRAFT). (n.d.). *Core Cybersecurity Feature Baseline for Securable IoT Devices*. Retrieved from https://csrc.nist.gov/publications/detail/nistir/8259/draft
4. NISTIR 8228. (2019). *Considerations for Managing Internet of Things (IoT) Cybersecurity and Privacy Risks*. Retrieved from: https://nvlpubs.nist.gov/nistpubs/ir/2019/NIST.IR.8228.pdf
5. BlockchainDefinition.com. (2018, August 2). Retrieved from https://www.bankrate.com/glossary/b/blockchain/
6. Butcher, J. R. and Blakey, C. M. (2019). Cybersecurity Tech Basics: Blockchain Technology Cyber Risks and Issues: Overview. Retrieved from https://www.steptoe.com/images/content/1/8/v2/189187/Cybersecurity-Tech-Basics-Blockchain-Technology-Cyber-Risks-and.pdf
7. Gemalto. (2018, December 4). Blockchain Security: 3 Ways to Secure Your Blockchain. Retrieved from https://blog.gemalto.com/security/2018/12/04/blockchain-security-3-ways-to-secure-your-blockchain/
8. REST API Tutorial. (2017, June 5). What Is REST: Learn to Create Timeless RESTful APIs. Retrieved from https://restfulapi.net/
9. REST API Tutorial. (2018, July 20). REST API Security Essentials. Retrieved from https://restfulapi.net/security-essentials/
10. Docker. (n.d.) The Industry-Leading Container Runtime. Retrieved from https://www.docker.com/products/container-runtime
11. Bocatta, S. (2019, March 21). The 4 Most Vulnerable Areas of Container Security in 2019. Retrieved from https://containerjournal.com/2019/03/22/the-4-most-vulnerable-areas-of-container-security-in-2019/
12. Souppaya, M. P., Morello, J., and Scarfone, K. A. (2017, September 25). *Application Container Security Guide*. Retrieved from https://www.nist.gov/publications/application-container-security-guide
13. NIST. (n.d.). PAS 1885:2018. Retrieved from https://shop.bsigroup.com/ProductDetail/?pid=000000000030365446&_ga=2.267667464.704902458.1545217114-2008390051.1545217114

14. Sjafrie, H. (2019, forthcoming). *Introduction to Self-Driving Vehicle Technology*. CRC Press. Retrieved from https://www.crcpress.com/Introduction-to-Self-Driving-Vehicle-Technology/Sjafrie/p/book/9780367321253

15. Balaban, D. (2018, December 17). Security Problems of Machine Learning Models. Retrieved from https://it.toolbox.com/articles/security-problems-of-machine-learning-models

16. Techopedia (n.d.) What Is Big Data? Retrieved from https://www.techopedia.com/definition/27745/big-data

17. ScienceSoft. (2018, April 4). Buried Under Big Data: Big Data Security: Issues, Challenges, Concerns. Retrieved from https://www.scnsoft.com/blog/big-data-security-challenges

Chapter 13

AppSec Is a Marathon—
Not a Sprint!

We've covered a lot of ground in the last 12 chapters!

You saw the changes that drive how software is conceived and created, how it's used, and what the security implications of these changes are. You learned that the drive for advancements in software drive the changes and maturity of processes used to create it, which further drives advancements in software and the perpetual cycle continues.

You learned that the world of software security is akin to a carousel ride, where the view changes with each revolution. You also learned that applying ideas, concepts, tools, and techniques from Agile are useful for building effective controls in the Agile development process itself.

Some Agile and Scrum purists may disagree with some of the advice that's been shown to work, but throughout the book we strived to offer the best practical advice possible, given what we've learned about Scrum and appsec as people are added to the mix.

We hope you learned that appsec is indeed a human-based problem to solve and requires special attention, treatment, and lots of patience to empower those on the front lines of software development. With this book, you should consider *yourself* empowered to help effect positive changes by applying the practical advice in your own unique environments.

AppSec is not one of those security control frontiers in which you can simply decide to enforce before the people who have to live with those choices are well prepared and on board with the changes affecting them. AppSec professionals and practitioners on the security team only have influence as the tool for change. Development teams don't report to the security team, so there's a lack of management authority over these people, especially when their own management creates conflicting demands on their time. You learned how to use this influence in positive ways that help to establish an Agile appsec foundation, strengthen it, and build upon it with deliberation to improve the people, processes, and technology that yield secure and resilient software *and* secure and resilient software development lifecycles.

You also discovered that appsec is never really *done.* Similar to painting the Golden Gate Bridge, once you're close to the finish, you get to start all over again. There is no Definition of Done for appsec controls—they're a living organism that requires constant attention to continuously improve, mature, and remain practical and achievable.

In wrapping up the book, it's important to remind appsec professionals and practitioners to remain current and continuously improve your own skills and currency in an ever-changing environment. It's vital to explore opportunities and make the time so you can take an active role in the appsec industry itself to capitalize on connections you make, talks and presentations you attend, volunteering efforts, and higher education.

13.1 Hit the Road

In this section, we're going to take a look at getting engaged with the Open Web Application Security Project (OWASP), learning about the Certified Secure Software Lifecycle Professional (CSSLP®) from (ISC)²®, and exploring some ways you can contribute to research and the appsec body of knowledge that will not only help you reach to your own goals, but enrich application security for the worldwide software development community, with an overarching goal of secure and resilient software.

13.2 Getting Involved with OWASP

As you have seen throughout the book, OWASP is at the forefront of application software security, permitting numerous opportunities to engage, join up, and volunteer your time and skills to projects that inspire you to help out.

OWASP advocates approaching application security as a people, process, and technology problem, because improvements in all of these areas are proven as effective approaches to solving application security problems and advancing the practices.

Joining OWASP as an individual, student, or corporate member opens up a worldwide network of appsec professionals, with local chapters in most major cities across the world. As a member, you can participate in over 200 active chapters, hundreds of OWASP projects, and millions of ideas waiting to become projects.[1]

OWASP organized its projects into three categories[2]:

- **Flagship Projects.** The OWASP Flagship designation is given to projects that have demonstrated strategic value to OWASP and application security as a whole. After a major review process, projects are considered to be flagship candidate projects.
- **Lab Projects.** OWASP Labs projects represent projects that have produced a deliverable of value. Although these projects are typically not production ready, the OWASP community expects that an OWASP Labs project leader is producing releases that are at least ready for mainstream usage.
- **Incubator Projects.** OWASP Incubator projects represent the experimental playground in which projects are still being fleshed out, ideas are still being proven, and development is still underway. The OWASP Incubator label allows OWASP consumers to readily identify a project's maturity. The label also allows project leaders to leverage the OWASP name while their project is still maturing.

You can find the list of projects and a list of local chapters at the OWASP website.[3]

13.3 Certified Secure Software Lifecycle Professional (CSSLP®)

The Certified Secure Software Lifecycle Professional (CSSLP) is the only certification in the industry that ensures that security is considered throughout the entire lifecycle. The CSSLP is for everyone involved in the software lifecycle with at least four years' experience. The following domains compose the CSSLP Common Body of Knowledge (CBK) that is focused on the need for building security into the software development lifecycle (SDLC)[4]:

- Domain 1. Secure Software Concepts
- Domain 2. Secure Software Requirements
- Domain 3. Secure Software Design
- Domain 4. Secure Software Implementation Programming
- Domain 5. Secure Software Testing

- Domain 6. Secure Lifecycle Management
- Domain 7. Software Deployment, Operations, and Maintenance
- Domain 8. Supply Chain and Software Acquisition

13.3.1 Why Obtain the CSSLP?

The CSSLP CBK contains the largest, most comprehensive collection of best practices, policies, and procedures to help improve application security across all phases of application development, regardless of methodology. The CSSLP certification course and exam not only gauge an individual's or development team's competency in the field of application security but also teaches a valuable blueprint to install or evaluate a security plan in the lifecycle.

13.4 Higher Education

Universities across the world have dramatically increased offering bachelor and master's degrees in information security, with some that allow students a concentration on application security; but no public university has a comprehensive program for software security as the SANS Institute offers. Throughout the book, you also saw numerous references to the SANS Institute and the work being done by their students. SANS offers a rich set of resources to help appsec professionals, and their courses are considered a gold standard in appsec education.

SANS offers a complete curriculum on secure software development. The curriculum consists of a set of seven courses, across three levels, that fit into an overall roadmap for professionals in IT security. Some of these courses lead to a certification, while others are electives in other overall courses of study. The courses are summarized in Table 13.1.

You can find out more about the courses and certifications at the SANS website.[5]

13.5 Conclusion

AppSec is a legacy problem that can't and won't be solved overnight. It requires everyone's active diligence, vigorous participation, ongoing awareness and evangelism, continuing education, and determination to make any dent in the problems.

Table 13.1 SANS Institute Curriculum for Application Security Professionals

Level	Course	Certification Available
Level 1	*Secure DevOps: A Practical Introduction* explains the fundamentals of DevOps and how DevOps teams can build and deliver secure software. You will learn DevOps principles, practices, and tools and how they can be leveraged to improve the reliability, integrity, and security of systems.	
	DEV522: Defending Web Applications Security Essentials is intended for anyone tasked with implementing, managing, or protecting Web applications. It is particularly well suited to application security analysts, developers, application architects, pen testers, auditors who are interested in recommending proper mitigations for web security issues, and infrastructure security professionals who have an interest in better defending their web applications.	GWEB
Level 2	*SEC540: Cloud Security and DevOps Automation* provides development, operations, and security professionals with a methodology to build and deliver secure infrastructure and software using DevOps and cloud services. Students will explore how the principles, practices, and tools of DevOps can improve the reliability, integrity, and security of on-premise and cloud-hosted applications.	
	DEV541: Secure Coding in Java/JEE: Developing Defensible Applications secure coding course will teach students how to build secure Java applications and gain the knowledge and skills to keep a website from getting hacked, counter a wide range of application attacks, prevent critical security vulnerabilities that can lead to data loss, and understand the mindset of attackers. The course teaches you the art of modern web defense for Java applications by focusing on foundational defensive techniques, cutting-edge protection, and Java EE security features you can use in your applications as soon as you return to work.	GSSP-Java
	DEV544: Secure Coding in .NET: Developing Defensible Applications DEV544 is a comprehensive course covering a huge set of skills and knowledge. It's not a high-level theory course. It's about real programming. In this course, you will examine actual code, work with real tools, defend applications, and gain confidence in the resources you need for the journey to improve the security of .NET applications. Rather than teaching students to use a set of tools, this course teaches students concepts of secure programming. This involves looking at a specific piece of code, identifying a security flaw, and implementing a fix for flaws found on the OWASP Top 10 and CWE/SANS Top 25 Most Dangerous Programming Errors.	GSSP-.NET
Specialty Courses	*SEC542: Web App Penetration Testing and Ethical Hacking* helps students move beyond push-button scanning to professional, thorough, high-value web application penetration testing. SEC542 enables students to assess a web application's security posture and convincingly demonstrate the impact of inadequate security that plagues most organizations.	GWAPT
	SEC642: Advanced Web App Penetration Testing, Ethical Hacking, and Exploitation Techniques. This pen testing course is designed to teach you the advanced skills and techniques required to test modern web applications and next-generation technologies. The course uses a combination of lectures, real-world experiences, and hands-on exercises to teach you the techniques to test the security of tried-and-true internal enterprise web technologies, as well as cutting-edge Internet-facing applications. The final course day culminates in a Capture the Flag competition, in which you will apply the knowledge you acquired during the previous five days in a fun environment based on real-world technologies.	

From the start, you've seen the folly and dangers of unleashing insecure, unreliable, and flawed software onto the Internet, but along the way you discovered how to avoid and solve most of the problems that will land you in hot water. Beyond the principles, tools and techniques, and advice offered to help you build secure and resilient software and systems that support the development of software, we hope you've also begun to shift your thinking toward a security consciousness that will serve you and organizations well, now and into the future.

By tackling your own software security and resilience, you'll instill—and maintain—the right levels of trustworthiness that your customers demand and deserve. You have seen throughout this book that software security requires a holistic, comprehensive approach. It is as much a set of behaviors as it is a bundle of tools and processes that, if used in isolation, will leave you with a false sense of security and quite a mess on your hands.

Effective security requires that you educate yourself and your staff, develop manageable security processes, and create a software development environment that reinforces the right set of human behaviors. It also means investing in the tools and expertise that you deem necessary to evaluate and measure your progress toward a holistic environment that rewards defensive systems development.

Our objective in this book has been to give you the information that we feel is fundamental for software that is considered secure and resilient. We hope that you take to heart with what we have offered here and bring it to life—improving the world for yourselves, your families, your organizations, your customers, and your peers.

References

1. OWASP. (n.d.) Membership. Retrieved from https://www.owasp.org/index.php/Membership#tab=Other_ways_to_Support_OWASP
2. OWASP. (n.d.) Category: OWASP Project. Retrieved from https://www.owasp.org/index.php/Category:OWASP_Project#tab=Project_Inventory
3. OWASP. (n.d.) OWASP Chapter. Retrieved from https://www.owasp.org/index.php/OWASP_Chapter
4. (ISC)². (n.d.). *CSSLP Ultimate Guide*. Retrieved from https://www.isc2.org/Certifications/Ultimate-Guides/CSSLP
5. SANS Institute. (n.d.). Secure Software Development Curricula. Retrieved from https://www.sans.org/curricula/secure-software-development

Appendix A

Sample Acceptance Criteria for Security Controls

Sample acceptance criteria for seven categories of application security functions or attributes.

Appendix A is offered as a small subset of pre-written acceptance criteria for application product user stories that have an associated business function, such as *log-in* to gain access to data and services. These items either cover a broad range of topics related to required security functions or describe a set of desirable security attributes that are observable as the application undergoes testing that leads to user story or Definition of Done completion. These are useful directly or are adaptable to organization-specific requirements for security and specific tools in use. Mostly, these are offered to you as a model for coming up with good acceptance criteria for a variety of user stories.

Category: Authentication	
Topic: Credential security	Acceptance criteria: The system stores the information used for authentication according to the firm's standard for secure storage of user credentials.
Topic: Replay attack protection	Acceptance criteria: The authentication process of the application protects the system from replay attacks by protecting the transmitted authentication information and examining the sequence of submitted authentication information.

(Continued on following page)

Category: Authentication (*Continued*)	
Topic: Protect credential guessing	Acceptance criteria: The system provides generic feedback to the user during the authentication procedure when an incorrect ID or password is entered. For example: *"Either your ID or password is incorrect."*
Topic: Reauthentication	Acceptance criteria: The system reauthenticates the user after the timeout period of inactivity is reached.
Topic: Protection of credentials	Acceptance criteria: The application masks the display of the password when it's entered or changed.
Topic: Password first use	Acceptance criteria: On first use, the system prompts the user to change the initial password and prevents access if the user does not comply. Also, it shall allow users to change their own password and/or PIN later on at any time.
Topic: Password resets	Acceptance criteria: The system permits users to change their own password when they desire or are required to.
Topic: Password aging	Acceptance criteria: The system forces users to periodically change static authentication information based on administrator-configurable timeframes.
Topic: Password expiry	Acceptance criteria: Prior to the expiration of password, the system notifies the user regarding the imminence of expiration.
Topic: Preventing password reuse	Acceptance criteria: The system prevents the reuse of passwords within an administrator-defined period. For example, when updating a password, a user will be prevented from reusing a password that was already used, based on administrator configurations.
Topic: Authentication data configuration	Acceptance criteria: The system enables authentication information configuration to administrator-specified rules for minimum length, alphabetic characters, and/or numeric and special characters.

Category: Audit	
Topic: Audit log	Acceptance criteria: The system maintains an audit log that provides adequate information for establishing audit trails on security breaches and user activity.
Topic: Logging of authentication information	Acceptance criteria: The system maintains the confidentiality of authenticators (e.g., passwords) by excluding them from being included in any audit logs.

(*Continued on following page*)

Category: Audit (*Continued*)	
Topic: Logging of specific events	Acceptance criteria: The system allows the administrator to configure the audit log to record specified events such as: • All sessions established • Failed user authentication attempts • Unauthorized attempts to access resources (e.g., software, data, process) • Administrator actions • Administrator disabling of audit logging • Events generated (e.g., commands issued) to make changes in users' security profiles and attributes • Events generated to make changes in the security profiles and attributes of system interfaces • Events generated to make changes in permission levels needed to access a resource • Events generated that make changes to the system security configuration • Events generated that make modifications to the system software • Events generated that make changes to system resources deemed critical (as specified by the administrator)
Topic: Action on audit log failure	Acceptance criteria: The system provides the administrator the ability to specify the appropriate actions to take (i.e., continue or terminate processing) when the audit log malfunctions or is terminated.
Topic: Archival of audit logs	Acceptance criteria: The system provides the administrator the ability to retrieve, print, and copy (to some long-term storage device) the contents of the audit log.
Topic: Log review and reporting	Acceptance criteria: The system provides the administrator with audit analysis tools to selectively retrieve records from the audit log to perform functions such as producing reports, establishing audit trails, etc.
Topic: Logging of specific information	Acceptance criteria: The system allows the administrator to configure the audit log to record specified information such as: • Date and time of the attempted event • Host name of the system generating the log record • User ID of the initiator of the attempted event • Names of resources accessed • Host name of the system that initiated the attempted event • Success or failure of the attempt (for the event) • Event type
Topic: Protection of audit log	Acceptance criteria: The system protects the audit log from unauthorized access, modification, or deletion.

Category: Authorization	
Topic: Access rights	Acceptance criteria: The system prevents access to system resources without checking the assigned rights and privileges of the authenticated user.
Topic: Access restriction	Acceptance criteria: The system restricts session establishment based on time-of-day, day-of-week, calendar date of the login, and source of the connection.
Topic: User privileges (discretionary access control)	Acceptance criteria: The system enables the assignment of user and group privileges to a specific user ID.
Topic: User privileges role-based access control (RBAC)	Acceptance criteria: The system permits the assignment of users to roles (e.g., regular user, privileged user, administrator) to permit or limit access to security features or other application administrative functions.
Topic: Resource control mechanism	Acceptance criteria: The system provides a resource control mechanism that grants or denies access to a resource based on user and interface privilege or role.

Category: Confidentiality	
Topic: Sensitive information protection	Acceptance criteria: The system is capable of protecting system-defined, security-related, and user-sensitive or private information (e.g., nonpublic data, protected healthcare data, etc.) from unauthorized disclosure while stored or in transit.

Category: Identification	
Topic: Unique user ID	Acceptance criteria: The system uniquely identifies each user of the system with a unique user ID.
Topic: Backdoor prevention	Acceptance criteria: All interfaces of the software that are accessed for performing any action have the capability to connect the activity to a user ID.
Topic: Process identifier code/ accountability	Acceptance criteria: For each process running in the system that has been initiated by a user, the system associates the process with the user ID of that specific user. Service-oriented processes are associated with an identifier code indicating system ownership or service ID ownership and are tied to an individual accountable for its actions while in use.
Topic: Autodisable user IDs	Acceptance criteria: The application automatically disables an identifier if it remains inactive for an administrator-specified time period (e.g., 90 days).
Topic: Security attributes	Acceptance criteria: The system maintains the following list of security attributes for each user: user ID, group memberships (roles), access control privileges, authentication information, and security-relevant roles.

Category: Integrity	
Topic: Replay attack protection	Acceptance criteria: The system provides mechanisms to detect communication security violations in real-time, such as replay attacks that duplicate an authentic message.
Topic: Integrity of logs	Acceptance criteria: The system protects the integrity of audit log records by generating integrity checks (e.g., checksums or secure hashes) as the log records are created and verifies the integrity check data when the record is accessed.
Topic: Integrity checks	Acceptance criteria: The system protects data integrity by performing integrity checks and rejects the data if the integrity check fails.

Category: Nonrepudiation	
Topic: Secure logging of specific information	Acceptance criteria: The system securely records information related to the receipt of specific information from a user or another system.
Topic: Time stamping	Acceptance criteria: The system securely links received information with the originator (sender) of the information and other characteristics such as time and date.

Appendix B

Resources for AppSec

These links are being provided as a convenience and for informational purposes only; they do not constitute an endorsement or an approval by the author or Taylor & Francis Publishing of any of the products, services, or opinions of the corporation, organization, or individual. The author bears no responsibility for the accuracy, legality, or content of the external site or for that of subsequent links. Contact the external site for answers to questions regarding its content.

Training

- Security Innovation's CMD+CTRL Training Courses
  https://www.securityinnovation.com/training/software-application-security-courses/
- Synopsys® Security Training and Education
  https://www.synopsys.com/software-integrity/training.html
- SAFECode Training
  https://safecode.org/training/
- OWASP Secure Development Training
  https://www.owasp.org/index.php/OWASP_Secure_Development_Training
- Security Compass Secure Development Training
  https://www.securitycompass.com/training/enterprise/
- WhiteHat eLearning
  https://www.whitehatsec.com/products/computer-based-training/
- Veracode Developer Training
  https://www.veracode.com/services/developer-training

- Secure Code Warrior
  https://securecodewarrior.com/
- SecurityJourney
  https://www.securityjourney.com/

Cyber Ranges

- CMD+CTRL Cyber Range
  https://www.securityinnovation.com/training/cmd-ctrl-cyber-range-security-training/
- Arizona Cyber Warfare Range
  https://www.azcwr.org/
- NICERC™ Cyber Range
  https://nicerc.org/pd/cyber-range/

Requirements Management Tools

- SD Elements
  https://www.securitycompass.com/sdelements/
- Jama Connect™
  https://www.jamasoftware.com/solutions/requirements-management/
- Atlassian Jira®
  https://www.atlassian.com/software/jira
- IBM® Engineering Requirements Management DOORS Next
  https://www.ibm.com/us-en/marketplace/requirements-management-doors-next
- aNimble
  https://sourceforge.net/projects/nimble/

Threat Modeling

- MS Threat Modeling Tool
  https://www.microsoft.com/en-us/securityengineering/sdl/threatmodeling
- ThreatModeler® AppSec Edition
  https://threatmodeler.com/integrated-threat-modeling/
- OWASP Threat Dragon
  https://threatdragon.org/login
- IriusRisk®
  https://continuumsecurity.net/threat-modeling-tool/

Static Code Scanners: Open Source

- Bandit
  https://wiki.openstack.org/wiki/Security/Projects/Bandit
- Brakeman
  https://brakemanscanner.org/
- Codesake Dawn
  https://rubygems.org/gems/codesake-dawn
- Deep Dive
  https://discotek.ca/deepdive.xhtml
- FindSecBugs
  https://find-sec-bugs.github.io/
- Flawfinder
  https://dwheeler.com/flawfinder/
- Google™ CodeSearchDiggity
  https://resources.bishopfox.com/resources/tools/google-hacking-diggity/
- Graudit
  https://github.com/wireghoul/graudit/
- LGTM
  https://lgtm.com/help/lgtm/about-lgtm
- .NET Security Guard
  https://security-code-scan.github.io/
- phpcs-security-audit
  https://github.com/FloeDesignTechnologies/phpcs-security-audit
- PMD
  https://pmd.github.io/
- Progpilot
  https://github.com/designsecurity/progpilot
- Puma Scan
  https://pumascan.com/
- RIPS
  http://rips-scanner.sourceforge.net/
- Sink Tank
  https://discotek.ca/sinktank.xhtml
- SonarQube™
  https://www.sonarqube.org/
- SpotBugs
  https://spotbugs.github.io/
- VisualCodeGrepper (VCG)
  http://sourceforge.net/projects/visualcodegrepp/

Static Code Scanners: Commercial

- Veracode Static Analysis
  https://www.veracode.com/products/binary-static-analysis-sast
- Checkmarx/Cx SAST
  https://www.checkmarx.com/products/static-application-security-testing/
- Synopsys® Coverity® Static Application Security Testing (SAST)
  https://www.synopsys.com/software-integrity/security-testing/static-analysis-sast.html
- Fortify® Static Code Analyzer
  https://www.microfocus.com/en-us/products/static-code-analysis-sast/overview
- WhiteHat Sentinel™ Source
  https://www.whitehatsec.com/products/static-application-security-testing/
- bugScout
  https://bugscout.io/en/
- Code Dx Enterprise for Application Security
  https://codedx.com/code-dx-enterprise/

Dynamic Code Scanners: Open Source

- Arachni
  https://www.arachni-scanner.com/
- Grendel-Scan
  https://sourceforge.net/projects/grendel/
- Wfuzz, The Web Fuzzer
  https://github.com/xmendez/wfuzz
- Subgraph Vega
  https://subgraph.com/vega/
- OWASP ZAP
  https://github.com/zaproxy/zaproxy
- Wapati
  http://wapiti.sourceforge.net/
- W3AF
  http://w3af.org/
- Google™ Skipfish
  https://code.google.com/archive/p/skipfish/
- Google™ ratproxy
  https://code.google.com/archive/p/ratproxy/

Dynamic Code Scanners: Commercial

- Veracode Dynamic Analysis
  https://www.veracode.com/products/dynamic-analysis-dast
- Acunetix
  http://acunetix.com/vulnerability-scanner
- HCL AppScan Standard
  https://www.hcltech.com/software/appscan-standard
- Fortify® Webinspect®
  https://www.microfocus.com/en-us/products/webinspect-dynamic-analysis-dast/overview
- Netsparker
  https://www.netsparker.com/
- Burp Suite
  https://portswigger.net/burp
- Qualys® Web Application Scanning
  https://www.qualys.com/apps/web-app-scanning/
- WhiteHat Sentinel Dynamic
  https://www.whitehatsec.com/products/dynamic-application-security-testing/
- SA Advanced Web Security Scanner
  https://secapps.com/webreaver
- Wallarm® DAST
  https://wallarm.com/products/dast

Maturity Models

- Building Security In Maturity Model (BSIMM)
  https://www.bsimm.com/
- Open Security Assurance Maturity Model (OpenSAMM)
  https://www.opensamm.org/
- OWASP DevSecOps Maturity Model
  https://www.owasp.org/index.php/OWASP_DevSecOps_Maturity_Model

Software Composition Analysis

- Veracode SCA
  https://www.veracode.com/products/software-composition-analysis
- Whitehat Software Composition Analysis
  https://www.whitehatsec.com/products/static-application-security-testing/software-composition-analysis/
- Synopsys® BlackDuck
  https://www.blackducksoftware.com/

- Sonatype® Nexus IQ
  https://www.sonatype.com/
- Open Source Management for Enterprise
  www.fossa.com
- Synk
  https://snyk.io/

IAST Tools

- Contrast Assess
  https://www.contrastsecurity.com/interactive-application-security-testing-iast
- Synopsys® Seeker Interactive Application Security Testing
  https://www.synopsys.com/software-integrity/security-testing/interactive-
  application-security-testing.html
- Checkmarx CxIAST
  https://www.checkmarx.com/products/iast-interactive-application-security-
  testing/
- ImmuniWeb® Interactive Application Security Testing
  https://www.immuniweb.com/products/iast/

API Security Testing

- TinFoil Security API Scanner
  https://www.tinfoilsecurity.com/solutions/api-scanner
- Wallarm® FAST
  https://wallarm.com/products/fast

Runtime Application Self-Protection (RASP)

- Imperva®
  https://www.imperva.com/products/runtime-application-self-protection-rasp/
- ShiftLeft Ocular
  https://www.shiftleft.io/
- Contrast Protect
  https://www.contrastsecurity.com/runtime-application-self-protection-rasp
- Microfocus Application Defender
  https://www.microfocus.com/en-us/products/application-defender/overview
- Signal Sciences Runtime Application Self-Protection
  https://www.signalsciences.com/products/rasp-runtime-application-self-
  protection/

- Trend Micro IMMUN.IO
  https://www.immun.io/
- TemplarBit Shield
  https://www.templarbit.com/shield/

Web Application Firewalls (WAFs)

- F5 Silverline® Web Application Firewall (WAF)
  https://www.f5.com/products/security/silverline/web-application-firewall
- Signal Sciences Next Generation WAF
  https://www.signalsciences.com/products/waf-web-application-firewall/
- Kona Site Defender by Akamai
  www.akamai.com
- Alert Logic®
  https://www.alertlogic.com/
- Barracuda® firewalls WAF
  https://www.barracuda.com/
- Citrix® Web App Firewall
  https://www.citrix.com/products/citrix-web-app-firewall/
- FortiWeb WAF
  https://www.fortinet.com/products/web-application-firewall/fortiweb.html
- NSFocus Web Application Firewall
  https://nsfocusglobal.com/web-application-firewall-waf/
- Imperva® WAF
  https://www.imperva.com/products/web-application-firewall-waf/
- Radware® Cloud WAF Service
  https://www.radware.com/products/cloud-waf-service/
- SiteLock Web Application Firewall
  https://www.sitelock.com/products/web-application-firewall
- Symantec Web Application Firewall (WAF) and Reverse Proxy
  https://www.symantec.com/products/web-application-firewall-reverse-proxy

Browser-centric Protection

- Tala Security
  https://www.talasecurity.io/

Index

Printed in the United States
by Baker & Taylor Publisher Services